Mahnaz Zahirinejad

**Iran's Strategy in Energy Relations with China and India
(1979–2010)**

PRACE ORIENTALISTYCZNE I AFRYKANISTYCZNE
5
PAPERS IN ORIENTAL AND AFRICAN STUDIES

Mahnaz Zahirinejad

# Iran's Strategy in Energy Relations with China and India
## (1979–2010)

IKŚiO

Warszawa 2016

# PAPERS IN ORIENTAL AND AFRICAN STUDIES 5

Publisher: The Institute of Mediterranean and Oriental Cultures
of the Polish Academy of Sciences
ul. Nowy Świat 72, Pałac Staszica, 00-330 Warszawa
tel.: +4822 657 27 91, *sekretariat@iksio.pan.pl; www.iksiopan.pl*


Series editor: dr hab. Krzysztof Trzciński, prof. PAN

Reviewers:
Prof. Girijesh Pant (professor, Jawaharlal Nehru University)
Prof. Hooshang Amirahmadi (professor, Rutgers University)


Volume editor: dr hab. Krzysztof Trzciński, prof. PAN

Technical editing and language editing:
Dorota Dobrzyńska


Layout, Graphics and typesetting:
MOYO - Teresa Witkowska


ISBN: 978-83-943570-3-0

Printed by:
Oficyna Wydawniczo-Poligraficzna i Reklamowo-Handlowa ADAM
ul. Rolna 191/193; 02-729 Warsaw

# Contents

# Preface

This study is based on four years of my PhD thesis research entitled *Iran's Energy Policy towards China and India: A Comparative Study.* Studying at the university of Jawaharlal Nehru and closely observing India's policy motivated me to use my research experience with regards Iranian foreign policy and to work on Iran's energy policy towards China and India. Iran was subject to US sanctions and changes in its relations with its traditional European energy partners resulted in it following a policy of looking more towards to the East. A result of this rotation in Iranian foreign policy was its attempt to make a deal with India via an Iran-Pakistan-India gas pipeline project.

Besides this, spatial relations between India and China and many years of conflict have resulted in valuable research by Indian scholars with regards Chinese policy. This has included a regular focus on Indian newspapers, journals and other materials relevant to the topic. Thus, I have had easy access to various sources of research and also many people who have done research on Chinese policy.

It is obvious that study in India has provided me with the opportunity to conduct such research. In addition to this, the supervision of Prof. Girijesh Pant, who has great knowledge in the field of energy and an amazing supportive personality, has proved to be of significant help.

In closing, I wish to express my sincere gratitude to my family, teachers and friends at the centre for West Asian studies and the university of Jawaharlal Nehru. Additionally, grants from the A.SK Social Science Award/WZB are gratefully acknowledged and the efforts of the Institute of Mediterranean and Oriental Cultures, Polish Academy of Sciences are greatly appreciated.

Mahnaz Zahirinejad PhD,
*Institute of Mediterranean and Oriental Cultures*
*Polish Academy of Sciences*

# Introduction

Iran is a major player on the world energy (hydrocarbons) market. It is estimated to hold 158,400 million barrels of the world's oil reserves and 33,500 billion cubic meters of natural gas reserves.[1] This provides the country with a strategic leverage in defining the global hydrocarbon regime. Although Iran enjoys a distinct status in the hierarchy of world hydrocarbon exporters, it remains critically dependent, and thereby vulnerable, to the world hydrocarbon regime because of its rentier character. The Iranian state draws 42.5% of its revenues from oil resources, accounting in turn for 80% of its exports.[2] The Iranian state thus needs a friendly global hydrocarbon regime to augment its energy power.

Iran needs a proactive foreign energy policy to enhance and augment its energy power to scale up its strategic salience in regional and global politics. Despite the Iranian government's efforts to cooperate with oil customers trying to increase its oil production, Iran's oil exports were falling for many years because of the country's nuclear program and its continued standoff with the United States. The US and UN imposed sanctions on Iran also had an impact on Iran's trade relations with Europe, with major engineering and plant manufacturers under pressure from the United States to stop trading with Iran. Under these sanctions European financing proved to be almost impossible, making it difficult to raise Iran's production capacity. As a result, some policymakers started advocating that Iran needed to search for new relations and partners in Asia.

As a consequence, Iran began to shift towards Asia, which was especially true of its energy sector that benefitted from Asia's emerging energy market status. Asia needed Iran's energy in its efforts to shift the global balance of power to its advantage. This means that Iran's energy could become the source of its power projection globally. It is this strategic dimension that leads to multiple possibilities that, in turn, create and define the scope of interdependence between Iran and the Asian players.

The huge possibilities are particularly demonstrated by the Iranian and Chinese relations. Iran's relations with India also create advantages, but it must be kept in mind that the Sino- Indian, Sino-US and India-US rela-

---

[1] OPEC 2016.

[2] Economic Cooperation Organization 2009–2010.

tions cast their shadow in the unfolding of the multiple exchanges. These factors make the relationship complex and interdependent. Still, the rich historical baggage does become a crucial factor in profiling the scope of the bilateral relations.

The present study attempts to analyze Iran's energy policy towards China and India (1979–2010), also focusing on the impact of international factors with help from Kenneth Waltz's Neorealism theory. Moreover, the dynamics of the world's hydrocarbon market can be studied through the eyes of economic independence because the market is determined by multiple transaction channels. The analysis of energy relations between the two countries can, therefore, be based on the theory of complex interdependence of Robert Keohane and Joseph Nye. In addition, the research is a comparative study that attempts to assess the nuanced yet defined divergence of scope the relationship between Iran and China, as well as Iran and India.

# 1.
# Theoretical framework

## 1.1.
### POST-COLD WAR THEORY OF THE WORLD

The theory of Kenneth Waltz, 'Neorealism / Structural Realism', had dominated international relations from its creation in 1979 all the way till the end of the Cold War. The theory explains general principles of behavior that govern relations between states in an anarchic international system. Kenneth Waltz, in his book *Theory of International Politics* (1979), describes the international system as an anarchy without an international government and authority over states and governments. Waltz argues that '… in this world of anarchy, which is self-help system, units worry about their survival, and the worry conditions their behavior, states take care of (themselves).'[3]

He writes that '…this world of anarchy leads states to be ready to respond to the behavior of other states, since there is no protector that states can depend on in an emergency situation.'[4] Thus, '…because some states may at any time use force, all states must be prepared to do so – or live at the mercy of their more militarily vigorous neighbors (and, as he explains), as among men, just as among states, the absence of government is associated with the occurrence of violence.'[5]

Referring to the role of the military, Waltz writes that the most powerful states are the most capable states of the system. All international regimes, therefore, directly reflect the politico-military pattern of capability.[6] Moreover, Waltz suggests that political integration among states is not easy and is possible only if it serves the interests of the most powerful states. Transnational actors, corporations or institutions are, therefore, politically unimportant in comparison to the states. It is the exercise of military power, threat and forces that allows states to survive and achieve their ultimate objectives. It is the military force that is ultimately neces-

---

[3] Waltz 1979: 105, 107.
[4] Waltz 1979: 102.
[5] Waltz 1979: 102.
[6] Isiksal 2004: 135.

sary for the state's survival.[7] According to Waltz, states can seek security only through the accumulation of military power in this self-help environment. '…To achieve their objectives and maintain their security, units in the condition of anarchy must rely on the means they can generate and the arrangements that they can make for themselves… Self-help is necessarily the principle of action in an anarchic order.'[8]

With the reunification of Germany, the collapse of the Warsaw Pact and disintegration of the Soviet Union, the traditional bi-polar military structure in the world was brought to an end. Given these new conditions, Waltz moved to describe this new phase of world politics. For instance, he predicted the rise of new European powers and the rampant nuclear proliferation across Europe.[9] However, two decades after the Cold War had ended, most central and Eastern European (CEE) states have joined the democratic European Union (EU). There has been no arms race and instead of a group of powers competing over the European spoils, the EU has become the common, peaceful project for both the Western and CEE states alike.[10] Thus, the realists' pessimistic assessment of the post-Cold War future of the CEE states has been proven wrong. Waltz's theory is, therefore, unable to account for the lasting great-power peace since World War II and the growing cooperation among states.

In these circumstances, some more liberal philosophers began to challenge the theory of realism, with Joseph Nye and Robert Keohane among them. Keohane argues that '…realism is particularly weak in accounting for change, especially where sources of that change lie in the world's political economy or in the domestic structure of states.'[11] Thus, when the realist perspective on international relations was failing to take into account many of the new aspects of interstate relations, Joseph Nye's and Robert Keohane's theory of complex interdependence emerged at times of world changes in the 1970s. Their theory provides a better understanding of the changing security concerns of the states.[12]

Keohane and Nye, in their book *Power and Interdependence*, highlight the interdependent nature of world politics. Their initial assumption in the era of interdependence is based on the idea that the very nature of international relations was changing. They argue that the world has become

---

[7] Isiksal 2004: 135.

[8] Waltz 1979: 111.

[9] Kissane 2007: 25–27.

[10] Kissane 2007: 25–27.

[11] Keohane 1986: 159.

[12] Isiksal 2004: 133.

more interdependent in terms of economics, communications and human aspirations. They claim that 'non-territorial' players, such as multinational corporations, international organizations and trans-national social movements have become the main actors.[13] According to Keohane and Nye, this complex interdependence is based on three main characteristics:

- The world actors are states and non-states with multiple channels of communication; interstate, trans-governmental and transnational.[14] This contradicts the realist notion that states only act as coherent, sovereign units.[15] These multiple channels reflect various levels of contact that the national leaders, both formal and informal, have with one another, continuously increasing the opportunity for dialogue and building of relationships between the significant interstate players. In addition, multinational corporations and financial institutions can directly affect the relationships between states.[16]
- The agenda of interstate relationships consists of multiple issues that are not arranged in a clear or consistent hierarchy. In other words, there are multiple issues with no hierarchy; military security does not consistently dominate the agenda.[17]
- Complex interdependence has reduced the role that a state's military force plays in international politics. This means that the military is not used when complex interdependence prevails on a set of issues.[18] With regards to this issue, Nye argues that '…using the military could have a negative effect on other economic goals.'[19] He explains this on the basis of four main clarifications: risk of nuclear escalation, negative impact on efforts to achieve economic goals, domestic opposition to human costs in case of a war and people's resistance in weaker countries.[20]

Keohane and Nye basically believe the new world to be a more connected place. '…As nations across the globe become more dependent on one another through international commerce, the Internet, multilateral organizations, and non-governmental organizations (NGO's), individual

---

[13] Isiksal 2004: 139.

[14] Isiksal 2004: 139.

[15] Brenner 2001.

[16] Brenner 2001.

[17] Isiksal 2004: 139.

[18] Keohane, Ney 1977: 25.

[19] Nye 1976: 130.

[20] Nye 1976: 130.

governments need to re-evaluate their foreign policy agendas....'[21] According to the complex interdependence theory this is caused by the rising interdependence among states, which can affect their relations.

However, as can be observed, the governments of many countries have begun to develop their foreign policy agendas so that they are closer in tune to the international relations theory of complex interdependence than to the realist theory that had dominated the world during the Cold War. This change is also more important for the great and middle powers with global and regional interests, such as China. In this light, we will review Iran's energy policy vis-a-vis China and India.

## 1.2.
## CONCLUSION

The theoretical framework, due to some important elements, such as the role of international factors in energy policy shaping, will attempt to explain Iran's energy relations and how they are determined by the new world politics and global economy with China and India. The theory of complex interdependence can help understand how the new world politics and economic interdependence determine relations between the oil and gas exporters and consumers, such as Iran-China and Iran-India. This is because the foreign policy of many countries such as China and India are more closely in tune with the international relations theory of complex interdependence since the end of the Cold War.

---

[21] Brenner 2001.

# 2.
# Iran's energy policy: an overview

It was on May 28[th,] 1901, that Mozaffar al-Din Shah (Qajar) granted the British subject William K. D'Arcy a 60-year oil concession in all areas of the country except for the five Northern provinces bordering Russia. D'Arcy agreed to pay £20,000 in cash and £20,000 in stocks in return for the rights to search for oil in southern Iran. If oil were discovered, the Persian government would get 16% of the profits. In 1904–1905, with bankruptcy threatening, D'Arcy got an extra £100,000 from the Burmah Oil Company (through the mediation of the British naval officials) to allow him to continue. By 1908 he was running out of money again, while the revolution that had erupted in Persia in 1905/1906 was making the project look increasingly uncertain. Burmah was threatening to pull out. So when the news reached London that the last test drilling near Masjed-e Soleiman in Khuzestan had finally produced a gusher of oil on May 26, 1908, D'Arcy and Burmah Oil were both delighted and much relieved.[22]

Iran's first crude oil cargo was lifted for export in 1912 and by 1914 there were altogether 30 oil wells drilled in Masjid-e-Suleiman.[23] World War I changed the situation by involving the British government directly in the contract. The aim of the British government was to provide fuel for its Royal Navy. On June 17, 1914, Winston Churchill (still a budding Liberal MP) became APOC's new customer. A deal was reached. In exchange for secure oil supplies for the British ships, the British government would inject new capital into the company and in doing so, acquired a controlling interest in APOC. Moreover, Churchill put before the Parliament a bold matching proposal: for £2.2 million, the British government could acquire 51% of the shares and two seats on the all-British board of D'Arcy's Anglo-Persian Oil Company. This could ensure the Royal Navy rock-bottom prices for its petroleum for 30 years, which subsequently proved to be the case. The British government also became a de facto hidden power behind the oil company.[24] D'Arcy remained its director until his death in 1917, but Churchill appointed two government directors (with vetoing power) to

---

[22] Axworthy 2008: 50–51.

[23] *Oil & Gas in Iran* 2012.

[24] *Oil & Gas in Iran* 2012.

the company's board. This new contract secured hefty demand for Iranian oil, which led to significant increases in oil production and exports, especially during the First World War.

During the First World War Iran was a front for many of the imperial powers and, as such, suffered from British, Russian, Ottoman and German invasions. The war's outbreak deepened the chaos, with the Turks, Germans, Brits, Russians, local revolutionaries, monarchists and tribes, and (later) Bolsheviks fighting each other sporadically. The British lost ground in 1915–1916, but kept their grip on Khuzestan and the oilfields. Oil extraction amounting to merely five thousand barrels per day in 1913 reached 33 thousand barrels per day in 1920. In the early years and up until the mid-1920s the majority of the oil was sold at a discount to the Royal Navy, with whatever remained getting passed on to consumers in Britain and then elsewhere to other parts of the world.[25]

In 1921, developments forced the British to accept Reza Khan, taking control in Tehran and impose a new, authoritarian government. In 1925, Reza Khan took the name Pahlavi and had the last Qajar deposed. At the end of the year, he made himself Shah. From the start, oil income was vital to Reza Shah, who wanted above all to establish proper central government control over all his territories.[26]

*Table 1. Oil Revenue and Oil Exports, 1919–1922*

| Year | Oil Rev. % (£.M.) | Rev. a % of exports values | Rev. a % of exports values | Vol. of exports |
|---|---|---|---|---|
| 1919 | 0.47 | 7.24 | 6.49 | 1106 |
| 1920 | 0.59 | 6.88 | 5.57 | 1385 |
| 1921 | 0.59 | 6.54 | 9.02 | 1743 |
| 1922 | 0.53 | 7.73 | 6.85 | 2327 |
| 1923 | 0.41 | 8.11 | 5.05 | 2959 |
| 1924 | 0.83 | 12.30 | 6.75 | 3714 |
| 1925 | 1.05 | 12.53 | 8.10 | 4334 |
| 1926 | 1.40 | 13.43 | 10.42 | 4556 |

*Volume of oil exports refers to long ton figures*
*Source: Bharier 1971[27]*

[25] Mohaddesa, Pesaran 2014: 4.

[26] Axworthy 2008.

[27] Bharier 1971.

## 2.1.
## TERMINATION OF THE D'ARCY CONCESSION

Reza Shah's government financed its development programs through modest oil royalties, customs revenues, personal income taxes, and state monopolies. During his reign, oil production royalties, although still low, quadrupled in terms of the Rial. Money was spent on defence and industrial development. However, Tehran was under extreme financial pressure with the inflation rate rising to nearly 45%. The Shah also needed a huge sum to meet his plans of railway and army development.[28]

APOC's profits in 1919–1930 were estimated at approximately 200 million pounds, whereas the royalties paid to the Iranian government amounted to no more than 10 million pounds.[29] The Shah thus moved to start talks to modify the oil concession in London in late July 1928.

On November 26th, 1932, the Shah cancelled the D'Arcy concession. But he was forced to patch up a new deal later, extending the terms of the concession to 1993 in exchange for a modest increase in his profit share to 20%.[30] As a result of the new agreement, royalties from 1931 and 1932 were recalculated, with the 1931 payment increased four-fold; from £306,383 (16% of the net profits) to £1,339,132 (based on volume).

*Table 2. Oil income 1923–1937*

| Years annual average | Oil exports quantity (mil. tons) | Oil exports value (fob*, mil. pounds)** | State oil income (mil. pounds)** | State income as % of oil export value (3/2) | State oil income as % of total state rev. |
|---|---|---|---|---|---|
| 1923–1926 | 3.5 | 13.0 | 0.9 | 7.2 | 13.8 |
| 1928–1930 | 5.0 | 23.7 | 1.3 | 5.4 | 15.1 |
| 1935–1937 | 7.8 | 26.6 | 3.8 | 14.4 | 16.8 |

* *Free on board before freight cost.*
***All values in the table are based on 1923–1926*
*Pounds sterling, i.e., they have been deflated by the UK export unit values.*
*Source: Badakhshan, Najmabadi 2004.[31]*

However, the ensuing rise in Iran's oil revenue still meant that the country's revenues were less than the British authorities were getting in taxes from

---

[28] Martin 2013: 130.

[29] Hershlag 1964: 205.

[30] Axworthy 2008.

[31] Badakhshan, Najmabadi 2004.

the company. For instance, with oil production increasing from 126 to 648 thousand barrels per day, British taxes throughout the period of 1940–1950 were twice as high as the royalties that were paid to Iran by APOC.[32]

So, although Iran's oil revenues rose, they still were not the main source of state income. Between 1926 and 1941, higher tariffs boosted annual custom revenues from approximately US $5.6 million to US $16.3 million. The government moved to launch a small income tax that replaced the local levies and enabled the government to extend its influence into the provinces. By 1941 the income tax provided annual revenues of US $10.8 million. Finally, the government relied upon its state monopolies on consumer goods, such as sugar, tobacco, tea, and fuel, which contributed approximately US $46.5 million to the budget annually by the early 1940s.[33]

However, the need for oil income grew with Iran's need to finance infrastructure development and modernize the army. The Shah thus asked London for a loan of 5 million pounds (in October and November 1938) and expected APOC[34] to help overcome its financial difficulties. The conflict between the Shah and the British government intensified and later became one of the reasons for the Anglo-Soviet invasion of Iran in 1941.

## 2.2.
## OIL NATIONALISATION

Mohammad Reza Shah Pahlavi (1941–1979) tried to change the oil contract to better support Iran's interest. In 1948, the British company secured 82% of the profits from each barrel of oil and the Iranian government just 18%. Iran's government was growing more and more dissatisfied with this arrangement.[35] While Iran's share of the income was so low, Venezuela's government was receiving 50% of its income from oil revenues.

Both sides of the conflict launched preliminary discussions on revising of the 1933 oil concession in 1948. As a result of these negotiations, Neville Gass, AIOC director, and Abbasqoli Golshayan, Iran's minister of finance, signed the Supplement Agreement on July 17, 1949. The 'Gass-Golshayan' agreement was sent to the 15th Majlis (Parliament) in its final days, which meant that the 16th Majlis had to carry out the relevant discussions. At this

---

[32] Mohaddesa, Pesaran 2014: 6.

[33] Ibp Usa 2009: 54.

[34] APOC became the Anglo-Iranian Oil Company in 1935 after the Shah decided that foreign diplomats should use the name Iran instead of Persia in all official communications – part of his policy to distinguish his autocratic, modernising regime from the limp decadence of the Qajars (Axworthy 2008). In 1954 it became the British Petroleum Company (BP).

[35] Carey 1974: 152.

time, direct payments to the government by AIOC from royalties, taxes and share of profits amounted to 1,885 million rial[36] in 1949–1950.[37] This meant that Iran's share from its oil revenues was still low. In fact, foreign exchange contributions from the oil industry to the Iranian economy amounted to 3.24 million rials in 1949–1950 and 3.680 million in 1950–1951. But the company's taxes paid to the British government were larger than the royalties paid to the Iranian government between 1949–1950. The company's taxes to the British government amounts to £51.40 million, whereas royalties paid to the Iranian government amounted to £16.03 million.[38]

Table 3. Oil production and direct payments to Iran

| Year | Production (1,000 metric tons) | Direct Payments (1,000) | Direct payments (per ton) |
|---|---|---|---|
| 1942 | 9,700 | 4,000 | 0.412 |
| 1944 | 13,718 | 4,500 | 0.328 |
| 1946 | 19,695 | 7,100 | 0.361 |
| 1948 | 25,574 | 18,700* | (0.360)* 0.731 |
| 1950 | 32,532 | 32,500** | (0.492)** 0.999 |

\* This figure comprises the sum of £9.2 million received by Iran as part of the 1933 oil agreement and the sum of £9.5 million under the supplemental Agreement of 1949, which was paid to Iran following the settlement of claims under the 1954 agreement. Excluding the latter payment, the direct payments per ton for 1948 amounts to only £0.36.
\*\* Of this sum, £16.5 million was paid to Iran following the settlement of claims under the 1954 agreement.
\*\*\*Of this sum, £9.5 million was paid to Iran following the settlement of claims under the 1954 agreement.
Source: Issawi, Yeganeh[39]

During the election campaign for the 16 Majlis, many candidates, especially the National Front nominees led by Dr. Mohammad Mosaddegh, made the new oil agreement into a major campaign issue. And when the new Prime Minister, General Ali Razmara, reintroduced the agreement to the newly elected Majlis in 1950, Mosaddegh and his allies led a successful fight against it.

Mosaddegh and his supporters proceeded to draw up a bill to nationalize the oil industry and demonstrations in Tehran and many other urban centers indicated extensive public support for Mosaddegh and his plans to nationalize the oil sector. In November 1950, the Majlis Committee rejected the agreement, in which AIOC had offered the government slightly

---

[36] The national currency of Iran is rial.

[37] World Economic Report 1950–1951: 49–50.

[38] Mohaddesa, Pesaran 2014: 5.

[39] Issawi, Yeganeh: 1962.

improved terms. These terms did not include the fifty-fifty profit-sharing provision that was part of the other, new Persian Gulf oil concessions.[40]

In February 1951, nationalization of the oil industry had become a general plan. Razmara advised against it on technical grounds and was assassinated in March 1951. The oil was nationalised but problems emerged soon after the nationalization process. Oil production came to a virtual standstill as the British technicians had left the country and Britain imposed a worldwide embargo on buying Iranian oil. As a result, there was no oil income in 1952 and almost all of 1953, when the inflation rate oscillated around 20–25%.[41] Oil revenues declined in 1953 with production levels at only 28 thousand barrels per day, around 4% of the 1950 production levels.[42] It seems that the Mosaddegh government's efforts to cope with the situation proved insufficient. The country suffered from low income levels, particularly from oil, inflation and shortages.

Finally, a coup d'état was organized by Fazlollah Zahedi, an Iranian general who replaced Mosaddegh as prime minster, the British Secret Intelligence Service (SIS) and CIA agents working with anti-Communist civilians and army officers. The CIA, focused on the seemingly growing influence of the communists, received help from the British intelligence and planned, funded and implemented the operation, supported by Mohammad Reza Shah. Mosaddegh's overthrow, with absent support from other Iranian groups and non-Iranian actors in the coup led by the CIA, was the result.

Immediately after Mosaddegh's rule, an international consortium called the National Iranian Oil Company was created, with the Anglo-Iranian Oil Company as just one member. The consortium agreed to share profits on a 50–50 basis with Iran. According to the new agreement, 40% would go to AIOC (renamed the British Petroleum Company in December 1954); 8% each for the five US companies of Standard Oil (NJ), Socony, Socal, Texas and Gulf; 14% for Royal Dutch-Shell; and 6% for Compagnie Française des Pétroles (CFP). The four Aramco partners – Standard Oil of California (SoCal, later Chevron), Standard Oil of New Jersey (later Exxon), Standard Oil Co. of New York (later Mobil, then ExxonMobil), and Texaco – each held an 8% stake in the holding company. This arrangement was later modified in April 1955, when each of the major US companies gave up 1% of their holdings, so that a 5% share could be made available for the nine smaller independent US oil companies. This led to the creation of a joint organization known as the IRICON Agency.

---

[40] *History of Iran 2006.*

[41] Majd 1995: 454.

[42] Mohaddesa, Pesaran 2014: 6.

The new Iranian government's policy led to an increase in oil sector investments. Consequently, offshore sites in the Persian Gulf, the Gulf of Oman and in certain parts of the Zagros Mountains, were put on offer. In 1959, a new section of the great northern Iranian desert, the Dasht-i-Kavir, was also offered.

Thanks to these investments oil production increased from 353 thousand barrels per day to 951 thousand barrels per day by 1959, 50% above the pre-nationalization levels.[43] Therefore, during the five year period of 1956–1960, the government's oil revenues amounted to $1228 million, compared with $483 million during the entire thirty-six year period of 1913–1949.[44] Oil exports became a large part of Iran's total exports (51% on average between 1936 and 1959) due to the royalty system in place, with the country's share of foreign exchange receipts from the oil exports relatively small. Non-oil exports continued to be the dominant factor in balancing of Iran's external account.[45]

In 1961, Iran joined other major oil-exporting countries to create OPEC (Organization of the Petroleum Exporting Countries), whose members acted in concert to increase each country's control over its own production and maximize revenues.

2.3.
IRAN'S OIL POLICY AND OPEC

Iran was not active on the international oil market until the establishment of OPEC on September 14, 1960. Along with Iraq, Kuwait, Saudi Arabia, and Venezuela, Iran (at a conference in Baghdad on September 10, initiated 'a unified stance' against the major oil companies, which had cut prices in the summer of 1960 without consulting with their respective governments. These countries alone could before hardly change anything on the global oil market, which was dominated by giant oil companies, but together, as OPEC, they now could. Thus, in the history of oil, the 1960s are known as the decade of OPEC's 'resistance' to the 'majors'.[46] In Iran, this caused growth in its oil income, so the Shah decided to reestablish the link between oil revenues and economic growth. Oil revenues increased from $10 million in 1954 to $443 million in 1962.

Beginning with 1970, the situation was gradually changing in favor of the oil producers. In November 1970, the Shah convinced the consortium

---

[43] See: Mohaddesa, Pesaran 2014: 7.

[44] Arman 1998: 11.

[45] Mohaddesa, Pesaran 2014: 7.

[46] Amirahmadi 1995.

to add nine cents to the price of a barrel of oil and to raise the tax rate on the company's income to 55%.[47] In January 1971, Iran took the leadership in negotiating the new price with the majors in Tehran. Iran argued that crude oil was sold to Western consumers at $12–$14 per barrel, with the Persian Gulf producers getting only $1 per barrel. Later that month, the Shah threatened the majors with unilateral legislative action if they did not agree on the new price with OPEC.[48] The power of OPEC grew further and made it possible to get the majors to agree to another rise in crude prices by 8.4% in January 1972 and by 10% more in June 1973 to compensate for the two-time dollar devaluation.[49]

Finally, the Shah announced that the 1954 operating agreement between the consortium of oil companies and Iran would not be renewed when it expires in 1979. Accordingly, on March 22, 1973, the consortium was transformed into a service company paid by the government for its work. In exchange it received guaranteed delivery of crude oil at the agreed price less 22 cents per barrel.[50]

While Iran was an important member of OPEC, it did not agree to participate in an embargo that was led by the Arab countries at times of the first oil shock. In 1973, members of the Organization of Arab Petroleum Exporting Countries (OAPEC, consisting of the Arab members of OPEC plus Egypt and Syria) had announced, as a result of the ongoing Yom Kippur War, that they would no longer ship petroleum to nations that had supported Israel in its Conflict with Syria and Egypt (the United States, its allies in Western Europe, and Japan).[51]

However, Iran, Iraq and some non-Arab producers, such as Nigeria, increased production to make up for some of the shortfall. Consequently, OPEC became increasingly politicized. From the very beginning Iran and Saudi Arabia were the two main contestants. Recognizing the significance of oil for the economy and national security, the Shah adopted a policy, which linked oil, regional politics, and economic growth. Iran's friendship with the United States and accommodation of the Oil Companies also contributed to the success of this policy approach.[52]

---

[47] Energy Information Administration, Iran 2008.

[48] Amirahmadi 1996: 50.

[49] Amirahmadi 1996: 50.

[50] Thompson 2012.

[51] Hasan 2009: 256.

[52] Amirahmadi 1993: 1.

## 2.4.
## OIL REVENUES AND MILITARIZATION

The link between oil revenues and arms purchases is well known. This can be especially seen in Iran's case after the country managed to increase its oil revenues during the Cold War. Iran was in a strategic position not only because of its relationship with the Western countries, but also because it had a long border with the Soviet Union.

At this time, Iran's oil revenues were up and the country no longer had to pay out about $100 million per year. So it could afford new weapons. Since it was no longer getting new arms under military grants but was paying for them from its oil revenues, Iran was also able to diversify its sources of supply.[53]

Military spending in this period (1955–1968) was growing smoothly. Between 1954 and 1965, the US gave Iran $612 million in military grants, but with the oil price hike in 1973, Iran's oil revenues amounted to around $20 billion annually, creating a supply of resources that an economy of Iran's size and infrastructure found difficult to absorb.[54]

It only needs to be mentioned that the Shah's political aim was to enhance Iran's role in the Persian Gulf. He used the oil revenues to expand and equip the Iranian army, air force, and navy. He wanted Iran, in the aftermath of the British withdrawal, to play the primary role in guaranteeing security in the Persian Gulf. This goal coincided with President Richard M. Nixon's hopes for the region.[55] Iran had become the gendarme of the region. While its military was never used in any major regional conflict, the Shah used its powerful image to deter his potential enemies and settle regional disputes.

The army mostly relied on the oil revenues for financing, helping Iran become a regional power. But the country faced an unstable, rentier-style economy.

## 2.5.
## FORMATION OF RENTIER STATE

Iran after 1951–1956 inspired Hossein Mahdavi (1970), an Iranian scholar, to invent the term 'rentier state' to describe the economic and political conditions of a given country. This was due to the fact that the nationalization process of the oil industry and the increased utilization of oil essentially had affected both the socio-economic and political structures in Iran.

---

[53] Gharehbaghian 1960: 87–100.
[54] Gharehbaghian 1960: 87–100.
[55] *Iran: Country Study Guide* 2003: 119.

Mahdavi described rentier states as states that receive substantial amounts of external rent on a regular basis. External rents are, in turn, defined as rent paid by foreign individuals, corporations or governments to individuals, corporations or governments of a given country. Payments for the passage of ships through the Suez Canal (after allowing for the operating and capital costs incurred in transit) are also considered external rents.[56]

Mahdavi believed that the massive amounts of foreign currency and credit generated by the development of petroleum flooded the state coffers and turned, at least some, oil-producing countries into rentier states. He noted that oil revenues received by the governments of the oil exporting countries had very little to do with output of their domestic economies and input from the local economies. In fact, 'only a few are engaged in the generation of this rent wealth', and most just in its distribution.[57] Thus, the input from the local economies – other than raw materials – was rather insignificant. The oil industry's main contribution was its ability to allow governments of the oil producing countries to embark on large public expenditure programs without resorting to taxation and without running into a drastic balance of payments or inflation problems that usually plague other developing nations. And since the oil revenues typically increase at a faster rate than the Gross National Product (GNP) of the local economies, the public sector of the oil producing countries tended to expand rapidly.[58]

This situation would not necessarily have to lead to some kind of socialism, but could turn into what could be considered as fortuitous 'statist'. In these conditions the government becomes an important – or even dominant – factor in the economy. This is not to imply that the local economies are not dependent on oil or that any cyclical behaviour in the oil industry (or oil prices) would not affect the local economies. But the dependence is indirect. It is through the expenditure side rather than through the inter-industry relationships of the oil industry with the rest of economy that the mechanism works.[59]

The creation of a rentier state can also lead to economic downturn caused by the so-called 'Dutch disease'.[60] This is because revenues from oil push infla-

---

[56] Mahdavi 1970: 428.

[57] Mahdavi 1970: 432.

[58] Mahdavi 1970: 432.

[59] Mahdavi 1970: 432.

[60] The 'Dutch disease' originates from a booming resource sector, which leads to a contraction of the manufacturing sector via a loss of competitiveness, due to currency appreciation. Extra foreign currency enters the country, is converted into local currency, and is spent on goods that cannot be traded across borders (construction, certain services and so forth). This makes other parts of the economy less competitive in international markets. In the countries with rentier states the way that 'Dutch disease' becomes apparent is different.

tion higher, making it harder for the country to develop a non-oil economy. As such, the Import-Substitution Industry weakens, with imported goods and services becoming more attractive. In these conditions, despite the fact that the manufacturing sector loses its competitiveness, the agriculture sector is also underfinanced, making people move to urban areas. It is important to note that the rentier economy is characterized by excessive urbanization.

The theory of the rentier state was developed further by different scholars, particularly by Hazem Beblawi and Giacomo Luciani (1987).[61] Beblawi preferred the term 'rentier economy' to 'rentier state', suggesting that the rentier state is really a subset of a rentier economy, and that the nature of the state is best examined through its size in relation to that economy and the sources and structures of its income.[62] Beblawi argues, '...a rentier economy is an economy in which rent plays a major role, and in which that rent is external to the economy.'[63] In addition, Beblawi and Luciani have added some other important subjects to the theory and delineated four characteristics that must be present in order for a state to be classified as a rentier state. First, the rentier economy, of which the state is a subset, must be one where rent prevails. Beblawi argues that there is no such thing as a pure rentier economy. He contends that the moment, in which an economy becomes rentier, is a subjective matter of judgment. Second, the origin of this rent must be external to the economy. In other words, the rent must come from foreign sources, which means the country receives substantial payments from the outside world. Therefore, domestic rent, even if it were substantial enough to predominate, is not sufficient enough to consider an economy rentier because economic rent is an income factor that only comes from production (labour), investment (interest), and management of risk (profit), i.e. internal forces of production. Third, attention must be paid to the fact that in a rentier state the majority are concerned with the consumption of the rent and only a few are engaged in the generation of rent. It is, therefore, a mistake to consider a country with high levels of foreign trade as a rentier state, even if it depends predominantly on rent, as is sometimes the case, for instance, with the tourism industry. This is due to the participation and involvement of the majority of society in the creation of wealth. Finally, the government must be the principal recipient of the external rent in the economy.

As mentioned before, this is because the oil revenues received by the governments of the oil exporting countries have very little to do with the production processes of their domestic economies.[64] It also, to use a phrase

---

[61] Beblawi, Luciani 1987.

[62] Yates 1996: 15.

[63] Yates 1996: 15 and see: Beblawi 1990: 85–98.

[64] Yates 1966: 23.

popular among the contemporary political scientists, 'brings the state back in' to the idea of the rentier state.[65]

**Rentier State and development**: In the 1970s, oil exports remained Iran's main source of foreign exchange. But the question is whether this helped the country develop. Iran's economic development started with the 'first oil shock', which led to growth in oil revenues in 1973. This development generated a major economic boom in 1973–1975. Participation of foreign capital in Iranian banking, manufacturing and military projects also increased substantially in that period. Most of these investments took the form of joint ventures of the government and the private sector, and were largely financed by the Iranian banking system.

Political and economic developments in the period of 1973 to 1976 saw the formation of the rentier state in Iran. It started with the 'first oil shock,'[66] which led to a rise in oil prices and a substantial increase in Iran's oil revenues amounting to over $20 billion in 1974 and $19 billion in 1975, an eight-fold increase on the 1972 figure. In 1976, oil production was at 6.0 million bbl/d and revenues reached over $22 billion. By 1977, over three-quarters of the Iranian government's revenues came from petroleum.[67]

*Table 4. Oil Revenue (1970–1978)*

| Years | Values of petroleum exports million US $ |
|-------|------------------------------------------|
| 1970  | 2,358 |
| 1971  | 3,494 |
| 1972  | 3,638 |
| 1973  | 5,617 |
| 1974  | 20,904 |
| 1975  | 19,634 |
| 1976  | 22,923 |
| 1977  | 23,599 |
| 1978  | 21,684 |
| 1979  | 21,684 |

*Sources: OPEC's Annual Statistical Bulletin 2004*

---

[65] Yates 1966: 14 and see: Luciani, Beblawi 1987: 51–52.

[66] The world oil shock of 1973 began in earnest on October 17, 1973, when Arab members of OPEC, in the midst of the Yom Kippur War, announced that they would no longer ship petroleum to nations that had supported Israel in its conflict with Egypt – that is, to the United States and its allies in Western Europe.

[67] *Encyclopaedia Iranica* 2013.

Growth in oil revenues led to higher employment rates, improvements in infrastructure and a rapid rise of per capita income in the rentier economy countries.[68] However, dependence on the oil revenues, coupled with the falling oil price in 1975, had a major impact in Iran and ultimately led to the 1979 revolution. Hooshang Amirahmadi in his book Revolution and Economic Transition: The Iranian Experience (1990) writes that falls in the oil price caused the following problems:

- 'The GDP growth rate dropped from 17.8% in 1976 to 7.2% in 1977.
- All economic sectors experienced significant declines, but the oil and industrial sectors, as well as real estate and construction, were the hardest hit.
- In late 1975, the government already owed its various contractors $3 billion in delayed payments.
- Private debt in the banking system increased to $19 billion and the banking system had accumulated a deficit of some $3 billion, of which $2.6 billion had been given in loans to the Iranian and foreign business owners who were already then fleeing the country (even before the revolution was fully under way).
- The value of imports dropped by 36% in 1978, but this was more than offset by a 67.2% decline in exports, leaving a $500 million trade deficit.'[69]

## 2.6.
## IRAN'S ENERGY POLICY AFTER THE ISLAMIC REVOLUTION

After the 1979 Islamic Revolution and subsequently the establishment of the new regime, Iran redefined its economy as well as its foreign policy. The economy became more state-dominated in terms of national resources, particularly in the energy sector, while the country's foreign policy shifted to an ideological approach towards the world. Iran adopted a hostile attitude towards Western countries, especially the United States. Consequently, Iran's energy policy faced some important changes.

Although for many years the National Iranian Oil Company (NIOC) was established to control oil production and exports, the Islamic Republic created a ministry of oil and put the NIOC under its tutelage. Based on the new oil policy, all NIOC's joint venture and service contract agreements with foreign oil companies were terminated in 1980. These changes were in full compliance with the revolutionary ideology, which argued

---

[68] Karl 2007: 9.

[69] Amirahmadi 1990.

that oil deals were serving the interest of the Western countries and US rather than Iran's national interests). This led to a total transformation in terms of bilateral and multilateral relations. As a result, Iran's oil production fell 75% between 1979 and 1981.[70]

The decline in oil production was aggravated by the US embargo and Iran-Iraq war (1980–1988). The outbreak of the war with Iraq led to physical damage of Iran's oil installations. The large Abadan refinery was strongly damaged by Iraqi attacks in 1980 and 1982. And although Iran's oil production sharply fell, the high oil prices, due to an internecine war between the two leading oil producers (Iran and Iraq), helped boost Iran's oil exports from over US $11 billion in 1980 to US $20 billion in 1983.[71]

In 1986, the need for weapons to continue the war, as well as the unexpected sharp decline in the value of oil exports to $5.9 billion dollars in one year had given the government a hard time.[72] So although the revolutionary government was committed to reducing Iran's dependence on oil and had a stated policy of restricting output to less than three million barrels per day, the situation forced it to revamp its oil sector.

At the same time, the Islamic Republic found itself isolated from the international community, which made its political position weak as far as the ability to achieve its goals was concerned. In addition to the isolation, Iran faced strong opposition to its war with Iraq. All Persian Gulf states, Jordan, Egypt, Morocco and major Western powers, such as France and the United States, supported Iraq militarily, economically and politically.[73] '...These international factors – the war with Iraq, the sharp decrease of oil prices, and the United States limited participation in the war against Iran – had led Ayatollah Khomeini to think deeply about the future and the survival of the Islamic Republic.'[74] Consequently, Ayatollah Khomeini decided to support the conservative and pragmatic figures and groups to find a way to end the war and save the revolution.[75] On July 18, 1988, Khomeini had to agree to end the war.

In the second decade after the eruption of the revolution, the Iranian government's approach had changed from idealistic to realistic and reforms started taking place. The new government, led by Ali Akbar Hashemi Rafsanjani, was moderate in its policy and acknowledged the need for

---

[70] Cordesman, Al-Rodhan 2006: 315.

[71] OPEC 2004: 13.

[72] OPEC 2004: 13.

[73] Metz (Ed.) 1987.

[74] Alnahas 2007: 126.

[75] Alnahas 2007: 126.

global engagement. Iran was in need of foreign investments to rebuild the country, which was badly damaged in the war with Iraq. But the government lacked the necessary finances to cope with this challenge.

As already mentioned earlier, the damage from the Iraqi air strikes and the reduced oil exports to 600,000 bpd during the summer of 1986, stopped the government's efforts to raise oil production with the average exports in 1986–1987 at around one million bpd, based on an output of 2 million bpd.[76] In addition, the low oil prices brought far less revenues to the country, which needed big sums to survive economically, socially and politically. This meant that it was very vital for the government to boost its oil output.

*Table 5. Oil revenue 1980–1988*

| Year | Values of petroleum exports million US $ |
|------|------------------------------------------|
| 1980 | 11,693 |
| 1981 | 10,047 |
| 1982 | 18,690 |
| 1983 | 20,273 |
| 1984 | 15,713 |
| 1985 | 13,012 |
| 1986 | 5,900 |
| 1987 | 9,400 |
| 1988 | 8,419 |

*Sources: OPEC's Annual Statistical Bulletin 2004*

Bigger oil production required foreign investment and the government had to embark on a reform path in both its domestic and foreign policies. The law governing foreign investment had to be revised as the Iranian constitution prohibited the granting of petroleum rights on a concessionary basis or as a direct equity stake. Rafsanjani tried to change the law to attract foreign investment, especially in the oil sector. He also tried to lure Western investors into developing Iran's oil industry. His government initiated some important changes in the oil and energy sectors. Some of them were as follows: signing agreements with the oil-consuming countries and private entities, increasing cooperation with OPEC and the oil producing countries, as well as creating new terms and rules for foreign investment.

As a result of these policies, Iran of President Hashemi Rafsanjani managed to reclaim its status as the world's second largest oil exporter after

---

[76] CIA World Factbook 1987.

Saudi Arabia, which exports about seven and a half million barrels a day. Iran's production was roughly 3.5 million barrels per day.[77]

After Rafsanjani's rule, the foreign policy of President Mohammad Khatami (1997–2005) rejected the notion of the clash of civilizations, believed to be based on the interdependence of economics, societies, and advocated a proactive approach. His policy led to major improvement of Iran's relations with all the major European states starting with 1998.[78] In addition, Khatami's policy managed to attract foreign investment. His government applied for membership in the World Trade Organization (WTO) and its faltering economy was desperate for international investment to help create jobs for the country's overwhelmingly young population.

In addition, Khatami benefited from a change in sentiment on the part of the United States, whose sanctions were the principal US instrument containing Iran. Faced with intense European hostility, in the spring of 1998, the United States modified its policy, a change that had been at work since October 1997, namely refrained from threatening with a secondary boycott over European investment in Iranian oil and gas projects.[79] And even though this decision had little to do with developments in Iran, it led to some agreement with oil companies investing in Iran's oil and gas sectors.

This policy changed, however, with Mahmoud Ahmadinejad (2005–2013) becoming president of Iran in 2005. Ahmadinejad's government was conservative in its foreign policy towards the West and most countries in and outside the region condemned Iran's nuclear program.

To understand the reason for Iran's shift from reformism to conservatism, it can be argued that although Ahmadinejad and the conservative groups were supported by power figures, such as Ayatollah Ali Khamenei, the Supreme Leader of Iran, high oil prices also played a key role in empowering the president to push ahead with his polices. Iran's total oil income in the first half of 2008 amounted to $54 billion, only $10 billion shy of its oil income of $64 billion for the entire 2007.[80] This helped Ahmadinejad's government conduct his policy towards the Asian countries.

It needs to be noted that Iran still needed to increase its oil income even though it was already high. While the oil revenues were up significantly, economic growth was down, unemployment grew, inflation was at unprecedented levels and most people had to work several jobs because the minimum wage was insufficient to counterbalance inflation. In those years,

---

[77] OPEC 2004.

[78] Rajaee 2004: 165.

[79] Sokolski 2000: 152.

[80] Press TV 2008.

according to a report published by the World Bank, '…the inflation rate was high, almost 25.7% in 2008. In addition, the unemployment rate was 12.5% in 2008.'[81] Thus, there was a need of new energy partners for the country.

*Table 6. Oil revenue 1996–2005*

| Year | Value of petroleum export million US $ |
|------|------------------|
| 1996 | 19,441 |
| 1997 | 15,553 |
| 1998 | 10,048 |
| 1999 | 16,098 |
| 2000 | 25,443 |
| 2001 | 21,420 |
| 2002 | 19,219 |
| 2003 | 26,124 |
| 2004 | 34,289 |
| 2005 | 53,219 |
| 2006 | 59,131 |
| 2007 | 64,901 |
| 2008 | 87,050 |

*Sources: OPEC's Annual Statistical Bulletins 2007, 2010*

## 2.7.
## IRAN LOOKING TOWARDS THE EAST

Former presidents Hashemi Rafsanjani and Khatami had tried to settle conflicts with the West, but Ahmadinejad, whose presidency coincided with a deadlock in negotiations between Iran and the EU-3 (Great Britain, France and Germany) over Iran's nuclear program, tried to establish closer links with countries in the 'East' under the title of 'Look to the East' policy.[82]

This policy moved forward '…when great changes occurred on the international and regional scene as well as within Iran. At the international level, there was a collapse of the bipolar system and US was making efforts to consolidate its status as the only remaining superpower in the world. Domestically, the government had adopted a conservative approach.'[83]

---

[81] The World Bank.

[82] Saghafi 2008: 2.

[83] Saghafi 2008: 14.

Changes in international politics led to shifts in foreign policies. In Iran, the majority of the radical conservative politicians considered moving towards the East as less risky than building relations with the West due to the latter's hegemonic tendencies. According to the Iranian government, the 'Look to the East' policy could serve Iran's national interests and allow it to break its dependence on the West and enforce a balanced foreign policy.

Iran faced two fundamental problems: a) political isolation and b) technological isolation. These were caused by Iran's foreign policy. The immediate consequences: political showdown with the West, particularly US, and in the region with its neighbors, intensified. At the same time, Iran heavily relied on its oil and gas revenue to support economic growth. Thus, in the process of formulating its 'Look to the East' policy, Iran's major considerations can be defined in terms of China, India and Japan, as the largest consumers of energy in the 21st century in the East Asian region. At the time when Iran was facing increasing international isolation, the 'Look to the East' policy could serve as a fine recipe for its stagnated oil business and the Asian nations, mainly India and China, promised stable markets for Iran's future energy trade.[84]

Ahmadinejad's government, therefore, tried to solve its problems through its energy policy towards China and India, making no effort to come to terms with the West. At the same time, it should be noted that the Iranian government, which at that time had survived for 30 years without ties with a superpower and had withstood various sanctions, needed to make strategic relations with the East Asian countries.[85]

2.8.
CONCLUSION

From the preceding survey and analysis of Iranian oil history, it is clear that oil has played a vital role in the shaping its domestic and foreign policy. During the Pahlavi dynasty, oil revenues bolstered Iranian power projection both on the global oil market and in a regional strategic context. Not to mention that also in the domestic system oil became very vital. This may be the reason why after the Islamic revolution, the government retained the character of a rentier state. However, during the first phase of the Islamic Revolution the region faced strong Islamic radicalization, which was also export beyond Iran. As the result, energy lost its strong linkage with foreign policy and ideology dominated foreign policy. At this time, oil was seen

---

[84] Saghafi 2008: 14
[85] Maleki 2010.

more as domestic need. Under President Rafsanjani the previous linkages were restored. He changed foreign policy and paved the way for creating a favorable climate for energy on the back of increasing of oil revenues. Thus, Iran started reclaiming its place as an energy player on the global market. During the President Khatami period the linkage could be seen in even clearer terms. When Ahmadinejad came to power, the gas policy was boosted, followed by a policy reiteration towards Asia. This has been reflected in ties with China and India. This shows how understanding the decision making process in Iran's energy policy and examining the impact of important factors such as domestic policy and international factors is important. These factors will be examined in the next chapter.

# 3.
# Iran's Energy Decision-Making Policy

The Islamic Republic of Iran is the world's 17th largest country in terms of territory, comprising around 1,648 thousand square kilometers. Its total population was estimated at 70,122,115 people in 2005. Apart from petroleum, the country's other natural resources include natural gas, coal, chromium, copper, iron ore, lead, manganese, zinc and sulphur. Iran is a founder member of OPEC and a major player on the world's energy (hydrocarbon) market. According to OPEC, it is estimated to hold 158,400 million barrels of the world's oil reserves and 33,500 billion cubic meter of natural gas reserves.[86] This provides the country with a strategic leverage in defining the world's hydrocarbon regime.[87]

Oil revenues have for many years constituted over 95% of Iran's foreign exchange earnings, paying for most of its industrial inputs, food imports, and military purchases.[88] For many years, due to sanctions, the value of petroleum exports had declined, but this development led to changes in Iran's economic policy. The government tried to reduce the country's dependence on oil revenues since the Islamic revolution 1979. For instance, in 1986 and again in 1997–1998, the government decided to follow the examples of Kuwait, Oman, Norway and others in establishing an oil reserve fund. The goal was to smooth out the pattern of oil-dependent government expenditures and to escape the so-called 'resource curse.'[89]

Article 60 of the Third Five-Year Development Plan (2000–2005) called for the establishment, with the Central Bank, of a 'crude oil foreign exchange reserve account' for the purpose of stabilizing the government's annual budgets during the plan's life. The aim of the article was to depose of all foreign exchange income from crude oil exports over and above the figure specifically projected in the plan for each year, to that account. However, the third Economic Development Plan aimed at reducing the government's dependence on oil revenues to less than 12 billion dollars,

---

[86] OPEC 2016.

[87] Economic Cooperation Organization: 3–9.

[88] Amirahmadi 1995.

[89] See: Amuzegar 2005.

but it actually soared to more than 40 billion dollars in 2006.[90] It should be noted that Iran's state budget in 1998 was based on less than 71,000 billion rials, but the figure soared to 600,000 billion rials in 2006. In other words, while the country's oil revenues quadrupled over the 7-year period, the state budget grew eightfold in the same period.[91]

This highlights the importance of the decision-makers involved in Iran's energy policy and the key role that it played.

## 3.1.
## DOMESTIC FACTORS

Oil revenues naturally were at the center of power struggles and competition among Iran's various political groups, which tried to develop and increase their influence over the oil sector with the use of both legal or illegal methods. The role of political factors in the shaping of Iran's energy policy can be explained by the power structure in Iran, the role of the all-powerful Supreme Leader, the position of the president as well as the interests of the ruling groups. This chapter analyzes internal political factors that determine Iran's making energy policy. These include the roles of: the ministry of oil, Supreme Leader, president, interest groups and institutions, the Expediency Council, parliament, and the Guardian Council.

### 3.1.1.
### MINISTRY OF OIL

The Ministry of Oil (Petroleum) was established in September 1979 and written into the constitution of the Islamic republic of Iran. The Oil Act of 1987 placed all oil-related operations under the government's authority and specified the ministry of oil's functions.[92] According to the NIOC website, companies affiliated with the Iranian oil ministry include:
- "National Iranian Oil Company (NIOC Affiliated Companies National Iranian South Oil Company (NISOC) Subsidiaries, Iranian Central Oil Fields Company (ICOFC) Subsidiaries, Pars Oil and Gas Company (POGC) Subsidiaries, National Iranian Drilling Company (NIDC) Subsidiaries;
- National Iranian Gas Company (NIGC), NIGC Affiliated Companies;

---

[90] Bakhtiar 2007.

[91] Bakhtiar 2007.

[92] NIOC 2007.

- National Petrochemical Company (NPC), NPC Affiliated Companies, Petrochemical Commercial Company (PCC) Subsidiaries, Petrochemical Industry Investment Co. (PIIC) Subsidiaries, Bandar Imam Petrochemical Co. (BIPC) Subsidiaries;
- National Iranian Oil Refining & Distribution Company (NIORDC), NIORDC Affiliated Companies;
- Iranian Offshore Engineering & Construction Co. (IOEC), IOEC Affiliated Companies;
- Oil Industry Investment Co. (OIIC), OIIC Affiliated Companies;
- Oil Industries Engineering & Construction (OIEC), OIEC Affiliated Companies.

In summary, the ministry's main responsibilities include:
- Assuring proper management of the oil and gas reserves;
- Enhancing the local relevant technical know-how with the ultimate objective of achieving self-sufficiency and independence from foreign expertise;
- Supervising the oil, natural gas, refinery and petrochemical industries and managing relevant activities;
- Executive planning of major projects and allocation of necessary financing for capital investments and operations;
- Supervising all companies under the supervision of the ministry of oil and their relevant subsidiaries;
- Representing Iran in international petroleum associations and global energy markets."

Even though the oil ministry is at the center of the oil decision-making process, approximately 77% of Iran's oil resources are under the control of the National Oil Companies (NOCs) and specially NIOC with no equity participation by foreign, international oil companies. It must also be kept in mind that the oil ministry is symbiotic with NIOC and does not control it.[93]

## 3.1.2.
### NATIONAL IRANIAN OIL COMPANY (NIOC)

The National Iranian Oil Company (NIOC) is the fourth largest state oil firm in the world. It is exclusively responsible for the exploration, extraction, and transportation of crude oil, as well as sales of natural and liquefied natural gas (LNG). Once it delivers crude oil needed by the domestic refineries and manufacturing plants for their petroleum products, the NIOC exports its

---

[93] Brumberg, Ahram 2007: 2.

surplus production according to commercial considerations in the framework of the quotas determined OPEC and at the prices prevalent on the international markets. The NIOC also signs long-term contracts with foreign companies in order to exploit the national oil fields and export products. In addition, the NIOC exports natural and liquefied natural gas via the 'National Iranian Gas Export Company', one of its subsidiaries.[94]

The NIOC has had this power since its establishment in 1948. In the 1970s, '…oil was providing 90% of Iran's foreign-exchange earnings in the last years of the Mohammad Reza Shah's rule.'[95] This made the NIOC important and, as a result, it was able to develop and function as a modern integrated oil company.

Throughout the Shah's reign in Iran, the NIOC had been an instrument of the government. It was run as a commercial company and not a state-owned corporation, although all its shares were government owned. The NIOC was still operated under the close scrutiny of the government. The prices of its four main products – gasoline, kerosene, gas oil, and fuel oil – could not be changed without the approval of the Iranian cabinet. Considering the seemingly widespread corruption present in most aspects of Iranian life by the 1970s, it was remarkable that the NIOC was able to develop and function as a modern integrated oil company. This is not to say that the company was immune to the intense personal and political rivalries that afflicted the ruling elite.[96]

However, after the Islamic Revolution, the NIOC was placed under the direct control of a newly created oil ministry. Though, according to the constitution, the oil ministry should function in symbiosis with the NIOC and it does not have any control over it, the law is not clear on the institutional distinction between the NIOC and the ministry.[97] The NIOC under this supervision is still responsible for the exploration, production and marketing of oil and natural gas. However, for fifteen years after the establishment of oil ministry, the NIOC did not even have a managing director. As a result, all the prerogatives and authority lied outside NIOC and with ministry of oil.[98] In addition, the ministry's role as a policy maker was mixed with the operational side of the NIOC, the National Iranian Gas Company (NIGC) and other state hydrocarbon companies.[99]

Since 1990, minor improvements have been made thanks to economic and political reforms, such as the appointment of an NIOC managing di-

---

[94] Ministry of Commerce 2009: 112.
[95] Reference for Business.
[96] See: Zoghi 1997.
[97] Brumberg, Ahram 2007: 2.
[98] Bayegan 2008.
[99] Ghorban 2005.

rector, occasionally from outside the oil and gas industries.[100] However, the managements of NIOC, NIGC and the National Petrochemical Company (NPC) were in practice under the control of the oil industry. They were politicized to the extent that hampered their commercial development.

## Organizational structure:

According to the NIOC website, NIOC's General Assembly (consisting of the President, Vice President, Director General of the Management and Planning Organization, Ministers of Oil, Energy, Industries and Mines, Labor and Social Affairs, Economy and Finance) is its highest decision-making body. It determines the company's general policy guidelines and approves its annual budgets, operations, financial statements and balance sheets.[101]

The company's Board of Directors has the authority to approve operational schemes within the general framework ratified by the General Assembly. It approves transactions and contracts, prepares budgets. The board also prepares reports and annual balance sheets that are presented to the General Assembly. The board supervises the implementation of general policy guidelines defined by the General Assembly, and executes operations via the company's managing director.

In late 1998, the NIOC split its upstream sector into five producing units: NIOC South, NIOC Offshore, NIOC Central, Pars Oil & Gas Co. (in charge of all aspects of the offshore gas fields of North Pars and South Pars), and a Caspian Sea firm called Khazar Exploration & Production Co. NIOC South, decentralized under the holding company, has four geographical units: Marun, Karun, Masjid-e-Suleiman and Agha Jari. The NIOC has had many of its functions privatized, broken up, spun off and subjected to an influx of managers from other sectors of the economy. Yet the industry still seems to be operating in many ways as it has always done.[102]

## Subsidiary companies:

NIOC has established acceptable degrees of coordination within its organizational set up. According to information available on the NIOC website, NIOC's directors act primarily in the area of policy-making and supervision, while the subsidiaries act as their executive arm in coordinating an array of operations, such as exploration, drilling, production and domestic consumption. The NIOC's subsidiaries were as follows in 2007:

---

[100] Ghorban 2005.

[101] NIOC 2007.

[102] NIOC 2007.

Iranian Offshore Oil Company (IOOC)
Central Iranian Oil Fields Company
National Iranian Gas Export Co.
National Iranian South Oil Co.
National Iranian Central Oil Co.
Khazar Oil Exploration and Production Co.
Petroleum Engineering and Development Co.(PEDEC)
Pars Oil and Gas Co.
Pars Special Economic Energy Zone Co.
National Iranian Oil Terminals Co.
National Iranian Drilling Co.
North Drilling Co.
Iran Petro Development Co.
Ahwaz Pipe Mills Company
Petropars
Iranian Fuel Conservation Organization
National Iranian Tanker Co.
Exploration Service Company (ESC)
Kala Naft (London) Ltd. – procurement
Kala Naft (Canada) Ltd. – procurement
Naftiran Intertrade Co. (Switzerland) – trading& swaps
Iranian Oil Company (UK) – Rhum gasfield
Iranian Offshore Engineering and Construction Company (Joint venture with IDRO) (NIOC).[103]

The politicization of the NIOC, a process that has been affecting Iran's energy policy, stems from the constitution and the power centers that have played the key role, interfering in the oil decision-making process.

### 3.1.3.
### THE ROLE OF THE SUPREME LEADER

The role of the Supreme Leader, according to the Iranian constitution, is based on the ideas of Ayatollah Rohullah Khomeini, who positioned the leader at the top of Iran's political power structure. The Supreme Leader, elected by the Assembly of Experts, may be dismissed at any time by that body.[104] Apart from this, he has broad and nearly unlimited powers. According to the constitution, the Supreme Leader directly appoints the head of the Judiciary, Military officers, the Expedi-

---

[103] NIOC 2007.

[104] *Constitution of Iran*: article 110.

ency Council, a majority of the Guardian Council members, Friday prayer leaders and the head of radio and TV. He also confirms the president's election and the heads of dozens of political, economic, and cultural institutions.[105]

Since the Islamic Revolution, Iran has had two Supreme Leaders: Ayatollah Rouhollah Khomeini (1979–1989) and Sayed Ali Khamenei (1981–1989), who played a significant role in Iran's energy policy. Although the Supreme Leader is not mentioned in the constitution in the context of energy policy, there are different ways in which the Iranian Supreme Leaders use their power in various political institutions to affect Iran's energy policy.

**Political policy:**

The first and most important impact of the Supreme Leader on Iran's energy policy was made under Ayatollah Khomeini's leadership. Under Ayatollah Khomeini's leadership, '…the 1979 constitution of the Islamic Republic officially enshrined the concept of public ownership and state administration of oil under state control, specifying that mineral wealth be at the disposal of the Islamic government for it to utilize in accordance with the public interest.'[106]

Based on the new constitution, in 1980, all of the NIOC's joint venture and service contract agreements with foreign oil companies were terminated. The joint venture companies were wound up and regrouped under the Iranian Offshore Oil Company of the Islamic Republic. The Islamic regime even changed the names of oil fields with imperial connotations. For instance, Cyrus became Sorush, and Feridun became Foroozan.[107]

Meanwhile, the policy of the revolutionary government under Ayatollah Khomeini was committed to reduce Iran's dependence on oil revenues, so oil production was limited to less than three million barrels per day. The result was a cut in oil production from 6 million barrels per day to 1.662 million barrels per day from 1978 to 1981.[108] In addition, the disastrous war with Iraq combined with the deterioration of the global crude market after 1981 and OPEC export quotas left the NIOC in no position to expand production even if it had so wanted.[109]

**Economic power:**

One way for the Supreme Leader to expand his political authority is to extend his economic reach. Many economic institutions function under

---

[105] *Constitution of Iran*: article 110.

[106] Brumberg, Ahram 2005: 7.

[107] Reference for Business.

[108] Pesaran 1992: 101–125.

[109] Pesaran 1992: 101–125.

the authority of the Supreme Leader, but officially are considered governmental organizations. This is particularly true of foundations (Bonyad), such as the Foundation of the Oppressed and War Veterans (Bonyad-e Mostazafan), the Martyr Foundation (Bonyad-e Shahid), the Holy Shrine of Imam Reza (Astan-e GhodseRazavi), the Khatamol Anbia Company, and the Fifteenth of Khordad Foundation (Panzdah-e Khordad), which legally are tax-exempt non-profit organizations that are free of parliamentary or presidential control. These foundations were established based on Ayatollah Khomeini's policy.[110]

Meanwhile, the role of the Supreme Leader during Ayatollah Khamenei's rule grew through these foundations in the NIOC and oil decision-making policy for many different reasons. For instance, in April 2006, the Supreme Leader formally announced his approval of a plan to revise Article 44 requiring privatization of considerable state assets (although still ruling out privatization of NIOC).[111] Under the privatization plan, 47 oil and gas companies (including Petro Iran and North Drilling Company) worth an estimated $90 billion were to be privatized on the Tehran Stock Exchange by 2014.[112]

Following the Supreme Leader's announcement, Iran's oil ministry signed an agreement with Bonyad-e Mostazafan to sell oil in 2009. Participation of Bonyad-e Mostazafan as a non-private sector in NIOC was not considered a step towards privatization of the oil industry. In fact, it can only be seen as interference of Bonyad-e Mostazafan. It is clear that its duties will conflict with NIOC in the long term.

The leader also keeps tight control over the Islamic Revolutionary Guard Corps, which play a tremendous economic role. The Revolutionary Guards have exploited their favored political position to win business.[113] Based on their aims, under Ayatollah Khamenei's leadership, on June 7, 2006, the ministry of oil awarded a $1.3 billion no-bid contract to the Revolutionary Guards to build a pipeline to transport gas across Iran.[114] This contract infuriated private construction companies because it would offer the Revolutionary Guards an opening to the oil and gas sector, which would increase their stake in Iran's economic issues.

As mentioned earlier, the lack of power of some elected officials, such as the president, resulted in the increment of the Supreme Leader's role along with the foundations of his control of the oil ministry.

---

[110] *Bonyad-e Mostazafan.*

[111] Brumberg, Ahram 2005: 51.

[112] *Iran lists 21 oil companies* 2007.

[113] Khalaji 2009.

[114] Khalaji 2009.

## 3.1.4.
### PRESIDENT'S POWER AND OIL INDUSTRY

The President is the highest elected official in the Islamic Republic of Iran and is the second highest-ranking figure in the country. According to the constitution, the president is responsible for the 'functions of the executive', such as the signing of treaties, agreements, etc., with other countries and international organizations. He also deals with national planning and budgeting, as well as state employment affairs. He appoints ministers, governors, and ambassadors subject to approval of the parliament.[115]

The president has control over the country's foreign policy, the armed forces, nuclear policy, or the main economic policy of the Iranian state, but all of it is actually controlled by the Supreme Leader.

'...In practice, presidential powers are circumscribed by the clerics and conservatives in Iran's power structure, and by the authority of the Supreme Leader. It is the Supreme Leader, not the president, who controls the armed forces and makes decisions on security, defense and major foreign policy issues.'[116]

According to the constitution, the Supreme Leader is the top decision maker. But sometimes the power of the president can affect the decision of the Supreme Leader. For instance, Ayatollah Khomeini had the final say on state affairs, but during Ayatollah Khamenei's leadership, which coincided with Akbar Rafsanjani as the president, the center of power shifted to the president due to Rafsanjani's position.[117]

Rafsanjani, due to the government's deficit and his liberalization policy, tried to change the petroleum law to establish relations with foreign states and oil companies. As a result, in 1987, the petroleum law allowed for contracts between the ministry of oil, state companies and 'local and foreign individuals and legal entities.'[118]

The new petroleum law allowed for contracts with foreign companies under a buyback system, meaning that the foreign company provided all the financial investments and, at the end of the contract, gave up all the operating rights to the state company. In return, the foreign company received a share of the production at a set price.[119]

---

[115] *Constitution of Iran*: article 115.

[116] Jahanbegloo 2005: 6–13

[117] Khalaji 2009.

[118] Ceragioli, Martellini 2003.

[119] Reference for Business.

Based on the new law, many foreign companies signed agreements with the NIOC to develop the Iranian oil fields. The first deal under the buyback agreement dates back to October 1998. It concerned the offshore Sirri filed, operated by TOTAL and Petronas of Malaysia.[120] In the following year, Iran signed contracts with France's Elf Aquitaine and Italy's ENI/Agip to implement an oil recovery program at the Doroud oil and natural gas field. Iran also agreed to allow Bow Valley Energy of Canada and TOTAL to develop the Balal field, an offshore oil field with 80 million barrels in reserves.[121] Although the NIOC attempted to establish ties with U.S. investors, it failed in 1995 when US President Bill Clinton imposed sanctions against Iran.

Moreover, Rafsanjani indicated that he would aim to diversify Iran's oil-reliant economy. However, he failed to make significant progress in this area. What is more, during his presidency, '…NIOC had to answer to numerous authorities' politically.[122]

Finally, Iran's high inflation and some expansive programs, as well as the powerful economically-politically vested interests had created barriers for the Rafsanjani government's reforms.[123] As a result, Mohammad Khatami, as the next president, had committed himself to continue to reform and stick to Rafsanjani's policy in the oil sector.

Khatami's government insisted on stabilizing the economy. He launched a five-year economic plan in 2000 that aimed to privatize many of Iran's major industries, including parts of the oil and natural gas markets. Despite its worn out, outdated oil industry, the NIOC moved ahead to increase foreign investment and oil output. The increased earnings meant that the NIOC could be able to modernize its oil industry and invest in improved technology.

However, this policy resulted in creating associations between the oil ministry and one hundred affiliated or subsidiary companies. All the oil and gas projects were split between these companies. For instance, all the explorations, drilling and production efforts were previously concentrated under one director in the NIOC, but from that time on, there were ten to twelve companies making decisions and having a finger in the pie. Meanwhile, '…with the growing power of the oil ministry, the number of employees also grew. Before the revolution, Iran had a total 54,000 people working for the Iranian oil industry. In 2007, this number reached a colossal figure of over 180,000.'[124]

---

[120] Reference for Business.

[121] Reference for Business.

[122] Brumberg, Ahram 2005: 26.

[123] CIA World Factbook 2008.

[124] Bayegan 2008.

Based on the new energy policy, the NIOC planned to boost oil production to seven million barrels per day by 2015.[125] To accomplish this, the government needed foreign investments of around $5 billion annually.[126] During Khatami's rule, the oil ministry signed agreements with foreign oil companies. In October 1999, Iran made what it believed to be its largest oil discovery in 30 years: an onshore field known as Azadegan, located near the Iraqi borders in the southwestern province of Khuzestan. It was estimated to offer oil reserves of 26 to 70 billion barrels and had the potential to produce some 300,000 to 400,000 barrels per day for a period of 20 years.[127] On November 1, 2000, Japan earned exclusive negotiating rights to develop Azadegan in exchange for a $3 billion loan to Iran. Japan negotiated the agreement for a consortium of Japanese firms that included Japex, Inpex, and Japan National Oil Corp.[128]

It was at that time that criticism began to emerge from factions opposed to Mohammad Khatami's government. Khatami faced fierce opposition from his powerful opponents within the unelected official bodies of the state, which he had no legal power over and this led to repeated clashes between his government and these official bodies. For instance, the Guardian Council blocked several privatization proposals and launched an independent probe of irregularities in the NIOC and the oil ministry.[129] At the same time, the growing power of the Supreme Leader was shifting Iran's domestic and foreign policies from moderate and reformist to conservatism. As a result, Ahmadinejad became president.

Ahmadinejad, as president, started to criticize the way the oil sector was managed. His government launched 'total change' in the structure of the oil sector and 'fundamental' changes in contracts. It also criticized the 'buyback' system under which Iran paid oil companies that develop its oilfields.[130]

However, Ahmadinejad sought greater control over the oil sector and established the Petroleum Council to supervise the awarding of oil contracts. But Ahmadinejad's policy came under criticism by experts. They believed that his policy has increased Iran's economic dependence on oil revenues. Some of them argued that expanding the government budget and increasing dependence on the oil revenues was a serious problem for

---

[125] Energy Information Administration, Iran 2008.

[126] Energy Information Administration, Iran 2008.

[127] Reference for Business.

[128] Energy Information Administration, Iran 2008.

[129] Brumberg, Ahram 2005: 29.

[130] Bayegan 2008.

the country.[131] It seems that Ahmadinejad was at least successful in decreasing the role of the reformist groups in the oil industry, which had grown during the Rafsanjani and Khatami periods.

## 3.1.5.
### Role of groups and institutions

Socio-economic interest groups and organizations play a major role in the shaping and directing state behavior and affecting the decision makers at different times and in different circumstances. These groups want to protect their interests and meet their goals.

This is naturally also the case of Iran. The Iranian society has witnessed strong relations between the major socio-economic interest groups and organizations – conservative clerics and bazaar – which would lead to the revolution and then to strong and powerful political and economic coalitions since the revolution.[132]

Bazaaris (traditional merchants), technocrats and reformists belong to the important groups that have played a role in the decision-making process regarding oil.

'…The Bazaaris, religiously based traditionalists, better defined as 'Hey'atis' – those who are bound by allegiance to a common cleric or mosque. Traditionalists do not only believe in Velayat-e-Faqih and the Supreme Leader, but they believe that the religious leaders' authority transcends the law and the will of the majority.'[133]

Some Hey'atis explicitly reject westernization and modernization, and prefer Iran's isolation from the international community. Some others, in contrast, prefer modernization and want Iran to have ties with the international community.[134]

The second group, including technocrats and reformists, is Western-oriented. It has played a strong role in the shaping of Iran's energy policy since the revolution.

'…Some of the technocrats and reformists graduated from Western universities, believe Iran's interests precede those of Islam. Some are globalist in thinking and most are pragmatic in outlook. The technocrats are focused more on written laws, and view knowledge, science and education as the most important prerequisites of progress.'[135]

---

[131] Nili 2010.

[132] Alnahas 2007: 51.

[133] Amirahmadi 2010.

[134] Amirahmadi 2010.

[135] Amirahmadi 2010.

Rafsanjani's presidency drew support from the Bazaar as far as the oil sector was concerned. However, some of his supporters belonged to the technocrats' group, yet also backed his oil policy. Although there was competition and many differences between the Bazaar, technocrats and reformists for more than 20 years, the decision-making process in Iran's petroleum sector was controlled by these three groups under the guidance of Rafsanjani and Khatami. That meant that most of the decision makers were eager to see qualified Western firms channel both capital and technology into this sector.[136]

In 2004–2005, radical groups that almost never had any role in the decision-making process in the oil industry, took power. Through Ahmadinejad's government, they lambasted the management of the oil sector and claimed that Iranian oil wealth was controlled by a single powerful family (the Rafsanjani family). It caused Ahmadinejad to say that '…the atmosphere ruling over our deals, production and exports is not clear. We should clarify it.'[137]

It is clear that Ahmadinejad would not have made such comments without the backing of the Supreme Leader, of whom he was a zealous follower and who had the last word on the important issues.[138] As could be seen in the Ahmadinejad period, some institutions, such as the Revolutionary Guard and the Dispossessed Foundation (Bonyad-e Mostazafan) strengthened their position in the NIOC. But despite the fact that Bonyad-e Mostazafan played an influential role in the NIOC's marketing division throughout the 1980s, during Ahmadinejad presidency Iran's oil ministry signed an agreement with it to sell oil in 2009.

It seems that radical groups have been successfully increasing their position in Iran's oil sector during the Ahmadinejad period. But there are still some official bodies, which have some power in the country's energy policy.

## 3.1.6.
PARLIAMENT, GUARDIAN COUNCIL, EXPEDIENCY COUNCIL

Parliament is an elected body that has the right to participate in Iran's energy policy. It is a unicameral legislative body with 290 members elected by voters every four years. Each member of parliament represents a geographic constituency. The parliament approves the country's budgets and can impeach cabinet ministers.[139]

The parliament has played the role of a watchdog of the NIOC, particularly its economics and energy committees. Its members have often

---

[136] See: Amirahmadi 2010.

[137] Bayegan 2008.

[138] Bayegan 2008.

[139] Jahanbegloo 2005.

politicized issues of oil management and used charges of corruption to block some of the NIOC's objectives.[140] This is due to the fact that the parliament has the power to approve all international agreements, contracts, and treaties. Approval of oil agreements and petroleum law issues is the parliament's responsibility.[141]

Iran's parliament introduces and passes laws, which are, however, ultimately approved by the Guardian Council. The Guardian Council, a highly influential twelve-member body of six clerics and six conservative jurists picked by the Supreme Leader, ultimately has veto power on all decisions made by the parliament. For instance, in 2001, a leading conservative ally of the Supreme Leader and former chairman of the Guardian Council, Ayatollah Ahmad Jannati, accused the oil ministry of diverting millions in state funds to foreign bank accounts.[142]

The Guardian Council's members 'can interpret articles in whatever way they want, and are thus free to approve or reject almost any interpretation of the constitutional law.'[143] The power of the Guardian Council to reject parliament-approved laws has caused conflicts between the two institutions. This is why, in 1988, Ayatollah Khomeini created the Expediency Council, which had the authority to mediate disputes between the two bodies. The Supreme Leader appoints each member of the Expediency Council, which, in turn, serves as an advisory body to the Supreme Leader. The Council is presently headed by former president Ali Akbar Hashemi Rafsanjani and the majority of its 34 members belong to Iran's conservative groups.

The Expediency Council is responsible for the approval of the country's main policies, including energy policy. For instance, in 2002, Iran's Expediency Council approved the country's 20-Year Vision Plan to advance the Islamic Republic of Iran at all national, regional and international levels. The plan was for Iran to become the region's economic, scientific and technical leader.[144]

The Expediency Council has also had its own privatization plan. Hashemi Rafsanjani, as head of the Council, believes that: '…There is a wide gap between the private sector and the government in this respect and we need to move towards real privatization and a free market economy in Iran.'[145]

However, the power of the Expediency Council has been reduced due to the conflict between the Supreme Leader (Ayatollah Khamenei) and the

---

[140] Brumberg, Ahram 2005: 26.

[141] *Constitution of Iran: article 77.*

[142] Brumberg, Ahram 2005: 44.

[143] Brumberg, Ahram 2005: 29.

[144] Vaezi 2010.

[145] Your Petrochemical News 2008.

head of the Council (Rafsanjani). This was caused by Ayatollah Khamenei's plans to take control of the other.

## 3.1.7.
### ENERGY POLICY AND THE SUPREME LEADER'S INFLUENCE

The Supreme Leader's dominance has grown and affected the decision-making process in Iran. The Supreme Leader exerts his influence over the government and the parliament because they have been controlled by the conservatives since 2005. The Supreme Leader's authority can be manifested through the implementation of plans, such as restructuring of the subsidy system, mainly in the energy sector.

The subsidy program, created after Iraq's invasion of Iran in 1980, sought to mollify a restive population and achieve 'social justice'.[146] However, continuation of the subsidy system in the past two decades has made people used to getting cheap goods at unparalleled anywhere else in the world levels, especially oil and gas. For instance, in 2009–2010, Iranians were paying as little as 38 cents for a gallon of rationed gasoline, less than for bottled water. Gas cost 10 cents per liter, while a liter of bottle water cost around 25 cents.[147] This means that the added value in oil, gas and electricity generation accounted for almost 25% of Iran's GDP in those years.[148]

It must be noted here that the Rafsanjani and Khatami administrations took considerable steps to end the multibillion-dollar public subsidies that dominated the economic policies of both presidents. However, their attempts even to reduce the subsidies ran into barriers.[149]

The plan was launched in expectation of higher revenues from the newly liberalized energy sector and government reforms, but it still raised the question why the previous governments were not interested in pursuing reform? Why was it that only Ahmadinejad followed through? To answer these questions it is important to examine the political obstacles that the governments of Rafsanjani and Khatami had faced.

**Leadership and parliament:**
In the early 1990s, technocrats under Rafsanjani were arguing for 'rationalization' of the subsidies, particularly the energy subsidies. Although Rafsanjani had planned to do this, the conservatives that controlled the

---

[146] Nader 2011.

[147] Nikou 2011.

[148] Guillaume, Zytek 2011: 2.

[149] Hooshiyar 2011.

Fourth Parliament opposed his plans to liberalize the economy and were able to successfully undermine them.[150]

Privatization, subsidy reform, foreign investment, and welfare expansion were again all considered by the Khatami administration between 1997 and 2005, but the Seventh Parliament had overruled these reform bills, arguing that they would boost inflation and put more pressure on the low-income social classes. The parliament then approved another plan to fix prices of goods and state services, which prevented the government from increasing prices of some goods, such as gas and gasoline.[151]

It is important to note that Ayatollah Khamenei, the Supreme Leader, was uninterested in backing Rafsanjani and did not attempt to stop the opposition to Khatami's plans in the Seventh Parliament either. At the same time, he had ensured that the parliament approve Ahmadinejad's bill, which was in practice based on Khatami's plan to restructure the subsidy system. When parliament was working on these plans, the parliament's research center had warned that removing price support would quadruple the price of gasoline and could cause similar increases for basic goods, creating an inflation rate of 60% or higher.[152]

The conservative parliament tried to delay changes by challenging the government's authority to decide on how to distribute savings generated from the subsidy cuts among the poor. In addition, Ahmadinejad demanded a broader bill to remove $40 billion in subsidies, but the parliament's speaker, Ali Larijani, a pragmatic conservative and rival to Ahmadinejad, called for a smaller, $20 billion subsidy cut.[153]

However, a premonition expressed by Ayatollah Khamenei was enough to change the parliament's decision, when he declared: 'I hope that between the parliament and the administration a desirable conclusion is reached on the implementation of the subsidy reform bill.'[154] After Ayatollah Khamenei's statement of support, Larijani appeared to change his tone, saying that the 'lawmakers would do their utmost to cooperate with the president.'[155] Moreover, following the parliament's approval of the plan, the Guardian Council, on January 13, 2010, finally approved Ahmadinejad's plan to allow prices of the up-to-now subsidized goods to convert with normal market prices over the course of the next three to four years.

---

[150] Alnahas 2007: 131.

[151] *High Oil Price.*

[152] Worth 2010.

[153] Worth 2010.

[154] Worth 2010.

[155] Worth 2010.

The reform plan caused the price of subsidized gasoline to soar to about $1.44 a gallon from about 38 cents a gallon. In addition, gasoline bought over and above the monthly ration would increase to about $2.64 a gallon.[156]

### Influence of the Supreme Leader via interest groups:

The other reason behind the accomplishment of Ahmadinejad's plan was his ability to bring some groups, such as the Islamic Revolutionary Guards, under his control. As already mentioned earlier, the Islamic Revolutionary Guards has been Iran's most powerful security and military player. They also control much of Iran's economy through the management or outright ownership of many industries.

The Islamic Revolutionary Guards as a group had expanded its influence in the oil and gas sector with Ahmadinejad becoming the president in 2005. This was possible thanks to the oil industry's privatization process, which created an opportunity for the Islamic Revolutionary Guards to increase business activities in the absence of foreign oil companies.[157]

It is also important to note that, although the Guards benefited from Iran's international isolation as the gatekeepers of an increasingly closed economy, some believe that

'...the Guards' ability to profit from their economic position was undermined by U.S. and international sanctions, which were designed in part to pressure the Guards on the nuclear program. Thus, the Guards believed that the subsidy reform plans could shift them back into a more favorable economic position and help secure their nuclear prerogatives.'[158]

This is how Ahmadinejad's plan received supported from the Islamic Revolutionary Guards. This shows how the Islamic Revolutionary Guards made Ahmadinejad administration's subsidy reform possible, while the earlier plan of Rafsanjani's government was criticized by the media, even when it just tried to remove subsides on bread. Rafsanjani had to thus abandon his plans for fear of unrest.[159] Even Mohammad Khatami, who advocated the need for economic, political and social reforms, and who got elected with the support of 69% of the vote, was afraid of mass protests against the reform plans.[160]

---

[156] Young 2010.

[157] Alfoneh 2010.

[158] Nader 2011.

[159] Eshagh 2011.

[160] Kazemi 2010.

The Guards' support thus meant that opposition and criticism of the subsidy reform plan disappeared. This move also made the Guards in 2010 into a major player in Iran's oil industry.

Thus, although the subsidy's restructuring process failed to offer any economic benefits, the process of its implementation clearly showed that the Supreme Leaders had control over the country.

### 3.1.8.
PRODUCTION AND CONSUMPTION OF IRAN'S OIL AND GAS

In addition to the structure of the decision-making process in Iran, other factors, such as production and consumption capacity, also determine the country's oil policy. These factors are especially important in the context of oil exports. For instance, some had predicted that Iran's exports would end up falling. In 2006, Roger Stern[161] claimed that, 'in absence of any policy change by the Islamic Republic, Iran's oil exports would decline to zero by 2014–2015'. He has considered the energy subsidies, hostility to foreign investment, and inefficiencies of its state-planned economy as the main factors that would harm the country oil exports.[162] Although this is not the only view on the subject out there, Stern's idea is important to consider due to the rising domestic consumption and falling exports, exacerbated by lower production levels.

Iran had 40 producing fields, 27 onshore and 13 offshore, with the majority of crude oil reserves located in the southwestern Khuzestan region near the Iraqi border.[163] Iran produced 6 million bbl/d of crude oil in 1974, but has been unable to produce at that level since the 1979 revolution due to a combination of war, limited investment, sanctions, and a high rate of natural decline in Iran's mature oil fields. Iran's fields have a natural annual decline rate estimated at 8% onshore and 11% offshore, while the Iranian recovery rates were 20–25%. Based on data in 2007, it was estimated that 400,000 to 700,000 bbl/d of crude production would be lost annually due to declines in the mature oil fields.[164]

In fact, in 2007, Iran produced approximately 4.1 million bbl/d in total liquids, of which roughly 3.8 million bbl/d was crude oil, equal to about 4.5% of the global production. Iran's crude oil production capacity was estimated to be at 3.9 million bbl/d in 2007. While oil production was falling, domestic

---

[161] Roger Stern of Johns Hopkins University present his idea based on a paper to the National Academy of Sciences.

[162] Kiernan 2007.

[163] Energy International Administration Iran 2007.

[164] Energy International Administration Iran 2007.

consumption kept on rising. In 2007, Iran's oil consumption was at about 1.7 million b/d, which left around 2.2 million b/d available for export.[165]

In 2007, former oil minister Kazem Vaziri Hamaneh said Iran faced a 'crisis' in its oil industry unless its consumption was curbed.[166] But the country was reluctant to take more drastic actions, such as eliminating subsidies altogether, given the low income levels. When Iran finally decided to take even a tepid course of moderate increases in the subsidized prices, spontaneous riots broke out and a few dozen gas stations were burned down, indicating that more drastic measures, though necessary in the longer term, would be politically risky.[167]

This led Iran to announce investment plans to boost its refining capacity and to increase the gasoline yield at its refineries. Sajadiyan recognized this problem and said: 'We are currently facing a dwindling production problem. Based on international figures, since our fields are in the second half of their lifetime, we are annually losing about 200,000 barrels per day in production.'[168] He said this was a 'a major challenge' faced by the National Iranian Oil Company in areas of exploration, development and exploitation of the country's hydrocarbon reserves.

Sajadiyan argued that 'to manage the energy resources, we must prevent pressure from falling before using any method to increase output'. He explained further that 'if the existing production resources were considered at 62 billion barrels and if we assumed that: 1. production and consumption would remain constant; and 2. annual output would fall by 2% against a 2% rise in demand, our country would have to import crude oil, respectively, after 40 and 25 years.'[169] He also described other related challenges and mechanisms.

However, Iran planned to increase its oil production capacity to over 4.5 million bbl/d by 2010 and 5 million bbl/d after 2015, but foreign assistance would be necessary to achieve these goals. It should also be noted that foreign investment in Iran's energy sector has been affected by international unease related to the US economic sanctions since 2006. In addition, according to the IEA 2008 Medium-Term Oil Market Report, it was predicated that Iran would not be able to expand its oil production capacity through 2013.[170]

---

[165] Energy International Administration Iran 2007.

[166] Bakhtiar 2007.

[167] Bakhtiar 2007.

[168] Sajadiyan 2009.

[169] Sajadiyan 2009.

[170] Sajadiyan 2009.

Due to Iran's big gas reserves, it has been argued that gas could be made into a strategic element into the country's energy policy. Based on this, gas would become an alternative to oil in Iran's energy policy. Gas could then become an important part of Iran's policy at some point.

Iran also wanted to gradually substitute its domestic use of oil products with gas. This would free up some of the almost 1.7 million bpd crude oil consumed internally for exports (to reach some of the goals listed in the next section) and attract energy intensive industries o Iran. This could lead to a transfer of knowledge and technology, but also create a supply chain within the country, creating jobs and increasing revenues.[171]

Iran's gas reserves are mainly based on independent gas fields, gas caps and associated gas, produced together with oil. Consequently, part of the country's gas reserves are geared to oil production and gas caps cannot be utilized for some time. Nevertheless, Iran is one of the leading players in the world when it comes to gas reserves and there is still potential for future discoveries.[172]

Iran was producing around 8% of the global gas production in 2007 and was expected to be able to produce five times more, on par with the US and Russia for over 40 years. So there is no major constraint on reserves and Iran must find a way to increase its gas production and utilization.[173] This means that gas might replace Iran's petroleum products in a way that frees its oil reserves for export purposes. Maintaining Iran's oil production also depends on a massive gas injection into the old reservoirs.[174]

*Table 7: Gas production 1995–2005 (billion cubic meters)*

| Year | Production | Consumption | Balance |
|------|------------|-------------|---------|
| 1995 | 35.3 | 35.2 | 0.2 |
| 2000 | 60.2 | 62.9 | -2.7 |
| 2005 | 87.0 | 88.5 | -1.5 |

*Source: EIA International Petroleum Monthly (1995–2005)*

## 3.2.
## GEOPOLITICAL OPPORTUNITIES AND INTERNATIONAL FACTORS

Iran's energy policy is not only determined by internal political and eco-nomic issues. It is also the final product of elements, such as geopolitics

---

[171] See: Ghezelbash 2005: 6–13.

[172] Ghorban 2005.

[173] Ghorban 2005.

[174] Ghorban 2005.

and international relations. What is more, international factors seem to play an ever more important role in Iran's energy policy.

## 3.2.1.
### GEOPOLITICS OF IRAN

Iran is located at a crossroads between the East and the West, and, at the proximity of the Eurasia Heartland, is the only country that connects two energy resource-rich areas of the Persian Gulf and Caspian Sea.

**Persian Gulf:**
The Persian Gulf is one of the most strategic waterways in the world due to its importance in oil transport. It has 715 billion barrels of proven oil reserves, around 57% of the world's reserves, and 2,462 Tcf (trillion cubic feet) of natural gas reserves, 45% of the world's.[175]

The Persian Gulf countries (Bahrain, Iran, Iraq, Kuwait, Qatar, Saudi Arabia, and the United Arab Emirates) produce nearly 30% of the world's oil. Oil flows through the Strait of Hormuz account for roughly 40% of all the world-traded oil, and the 17 MMBD or more of oil that normally are shipped through the Strait of Hormuz goes eastwards to Asia (especially Japan, China, and India) and westwards (via the Suez Canal, the Sumed pipeline).[176]

Iran's coastline is particularly important. The tanker and shipping routes pass very close to Iran's land mass, as well as the islands that it controls in the Persian Gulf and its major naval bases.[177] At its narrowest point (the Strait of Hormuz), the Gulf narrows down to only 34 miles, with Iran to its North and Oman to its south. The key passages through the Strait consist of 2-mile wide channels for inbound and outbound tanker traffic, as well as a 2-mile wide buffer zone. Thus, Iran is a key factor for stability in the region and the Persian Gulf. Iran can play an important role in the region and the world, as well as on the global oil market. Roughly 90% of all Persian Gulf oil leaves the region on tankers that must pass through this narrow waterway opposite the Iranian coast, while the land pipelines do not provide sufficient alternative export routes.[178]

A blockage of the strait would pose a great threat to the flow of Persian Gulf oil, especially at times of lower global capacity and higher oil prices. Iran has control of the Hormuz and most oil leaving this region passes through it.

---

[175] See: Mohammadi 2003.
[176] Cordesman 2007: 2.
[177] Cordesman 2007: 23.
[178] Talmadge 2008: 82–117.

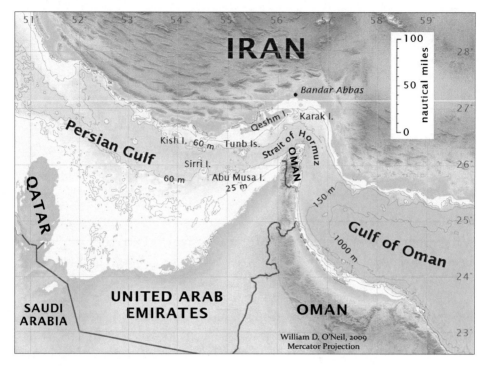

Map 1. The Strait of Hormuz
Source: Compiled and drawn by William D. O'Neil, Mercator Projection (2009)

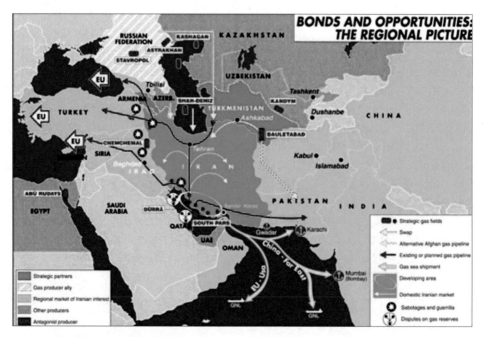

Map 2. Pipeline network via Iran
Source: Word Press 2015

**Central Asia:**

Iran has 8731 kilometers of territorial and maritime borders with fifteen countries. Links between Iran and the countries of Greater Central Asia include territorial borders with Afghanistan and Turkmenistan, and with Kazakhstan via the Caspian Sea. The Iran-Afghanistan border includes 945 kilometers of mountainous terrain that greatly assists drug traffickers.[179] This location has made Iran able to play a major role in Central Asia and Afghanistan. Geography favors Iran's relations with the Greater Central Asian states, since all these states are landlocked, and some of them (Uzbekistan) double-landlocked. Their shortest and most natural route to the open seas is through Iran.[180] Iran is also actively interested in developing transport infrastructure in Central Asia that will enable it to take advantage of its strategic location between Turkey and the Arab states in the west and South Asia in the east, and between the Caucasus, Caspian and Central Asia region to the north and the Persian Gulf to its south. However, in this policy, again oil and gas are the keys to the economic prosperity of the region but they must first be delivered to the high-income importing countries.[181]

Iran has an extensive pipeline network, to which pipelines from the Central Asia could be connected. The swapping of oil via the Caspian Sea is growing steadily and the capacity of the Neka-Ray pipeline inside Iran has been expanded to 170 000 b/d.[182] Iran also supports some of the following possible pipelines: the Tabriz-Ankara pipeline from Tabriz (Iran) to Ankara (Turkey), the Baku-Tabriz pipeline from Baku (Azerbaijan) to Tabriz (Iran) and the Tehran-Kharg Island pipeline from Tehran. Therefore, in Central Asia, Iran can also play a strategic role based on its energy relations.

Therefore, Iran's geographic location gives it the ability to transfer its energy resources through pipelines from its south, east and north to the European and Asian consumers. This is especially true in the gas sector because Iran has the second largest natural gas reserves in the world and gas has become a priority in the energy security strategies of the energy consumers.[183] In addition, Iran's geographic location provides it with significant geopolitical opportunities through the use of its oil and gas resources. Iran in the Persian Gulf has land borders with seven countries, while being one of the five Caspian Sea littoral states. This location not only provides Iran with a significant strategic posi-

---

[179] Maleki 2010.

[180] Dannreuther 2003: 32–46.

[181] Maleki 2010.

[182] Dannreuther 2003: 32–46.

[183] Dannreuther 2003: 32–46.

tion for becoming an energy transit route but also with major trading opportunities.[184]

Thus, in Iran's oil decision-making process, its geographic location as a best transit route between the oil trading countries has played a significant role. For instance, '…there is substantial potential for energy cooperation between Iran and the European countries, particularly Turkey.'[185] Examples of the Iranian desire to utilize this strategic position are the various pipeline projects executed or under construction. Iran has a gas export pipeline to Turkey and an import pipeline from Turkmenistan.[186] In addition, Iran via the Caspian Region Oil Swap (CROS) has exported crude oil from its Persian Gulf export terminals to its northern neighbors.

**The world's energy demand:**
An even large increase in the world's gas consumption is expected. According to the US Energy Information Administration, the 'total natural gas consumption worldwide increases 44% in the IEO2010Reference case, from 108 trillion cubic feet in 2007 to 156 trillion cubic feet in 2035.'[187] The world is, therefore, experiencing a rapid rise in energy demand and consumption. However, global markets also face a shortage of energy because of the sharp reduction of production capacity surplus and because of the increase in energy demand and consumption.[188]

Global demand for energy plays an important role in Iran's energy policy. Iran is a major player on the world's energy (hydrocarbon) market. It is a supplier of energy and this affects its relations with both the European and Asian oil consumers. This means that Iran's oil and gas resources, as well as its unique geography, have given it an important role on the global oil market. However, it must be kept in mind that there are also some political issues that can limit its position and role on the global energy markets.

3.2.2.
THE UNITED STATES SANCTIONS

In the mid-1970s, with a production level of more than 6 million barrels per day (mbd), Iran was one of the world's leading energy producers[189] and the

---

[184] Ghezelbash 2005: 26.

[185] Maleki 2007: 103.

[186] Ghezelbash 2005: 26.

[187] *International Energy Outlook 2010.*

[188] Vaezi 2006: 22.

[189] Rivlin 2006.

United States and Western Countries were its energy partners. The 1979 Iranian Revolution ousted the pro-American Shah (Mohammad Reza Pahlavi) and replaced him with the anti-American Supreme Leader Ayatollah Khomeini. On November 4, 1979, a revolutionary group occupied the American embassy in Tehran and took US diplomats hostage. 52 US diplomats were held hostage for 444 days. That was the start of the conflict between the two countries, followed by US sanctions against Iran and its oil industry.[190]

The main US reaction to the embassy hostage in Tehran was ending its energy relations with Iran. The US government responded immediately by issuing Proclamation 4702, imposing a ban on Iranian oil imports into the US.[191] The sanction was extended following the 1983 bombing of the US embassy and marine barracks in Lebanon. The United States accused the Iranian government of supporting terrorism due to Iran's relations with some Lebanese groups.

The US re-flagging of Kuwaiti oil tankers in the Persian Gulf and especially the shooting down of an Iranian airliner carrying over 200 passengers by the American navy in 1988 increased the tensions between the two countries even further. As a result, US President Ronald Reagan issued an executive order banning the imports of all Iranian goods and services worth a total of about $1 billion. US oil companies were also prohibited from importing Iranian oil into the United States for local consumption.[192] However, the US sanctions did not have a significant effect on Iran's oil industry in these years due to the fact that reducing oil production was part of Iran's energy policy.

There were many reasons behind the policy of reducing oil production by the Iranian government. The main reason was the influence of foreign policy on the energy policy. The approach of anti-Western and particularly US policy dominated the foreign policy agendas of the Iranian government and it impacted its energy policy. As a result, the Iranian government accomplished the following policies in the energy sector: 1) cancellation of all oil agreements with the Western states and their oil companies, 2) reduction of oil production, 3) attempt to reduce Iran's economic dependence on oil revenue, and 4) changes in rules about foreign investment and agreement with foreign states and oil companies.

This led to a reduction of oil production in Iran. Meanwhile, Iran's oil industry was damaged during the war with Iraq and oil production declined, lowering Iran's oil share on the global oil market.

Although between 1979 and 1985, Iran's oil exports were down, the high oil price that resulted from the war between Iran and Iraq – two main

---

[190] Estelami 1999.

[191] Franssen, Morton 2002.

[192] Estelami 1999.

oil producers – helped the government of Iran continue its revolutionary policy towards the US.[193]

However, the decline of oil prices in 1986–1987 and the need for weapons to continue the war, coupled with the unexpected sharp decrease of oil revenue to 5,900 million dollars in a year (Table 5), the economic sanctions and the political isolation imposed on Iran's trade with other countries gave the Iranian government a hard time in 1986.[194] Under these circumstances, Ayatollah Khomeini accepted the moderate group's view that the war had to end in 1987.

### 3.2.3.
### PERVASIVE US SANCTIONS

The sanctions ended Iran's energy relations with the United States and Iran moved to make up for this by building ties with European countries and Eastern Europe. As a result, the American oil companies, in competition with their European and Asian oil counterparts, lost the Iranian oil market. Under the pressure of the American oil companies,

'in late 1991, George H.W. Bush, as president of the US, allowed a limited amount of Iranian crude oil into the United States. During this period, not only were the American exporters doing great business in Iran, but American oil companies also became Iran's number-one customer for crude oil (most of which was shipped to their subsidiaries in Europe).'[195]

In 1995, there was a coordinated effort by the Israeli government to pressure the administration of the Unites States, President Bill Clinton, to pursue a policy of 'dual containment', with a special emphasis on sanctions against Iran and Iraq. The Israelis accused the Iranian government of three sins: sponsoring terrorism worldwide, opposing the Middle East peace efforts and developing weapons of mass destruction. A case in point was Senator Alfonse D'Amato's attempt to outbid the Clinton administration in support for Israel.[196]

Finally, the American Israel Public Affairs Committee pushed for comprehensive US sanctions against Iran, including sanctions against foreign companies seeking to invest in Iran's petroleum sector, and later the Iran and Libya Sanctions Act (ILSA) of 1996 (Libya had been added by Sena-

---

[193] OPEC 2004: 13.

[194] Alnahas 2007: 137.

[195] Alnahas 2007: 137.

[196] Fayazmanesh 2002: 227.

tor Kennedy because of the Lockerbie bombing).[197] The purpose of the bill was to reduce Iran's ability to export oil and gas, and access foreign capital and equipment for the maintenance and expansion of oil production. '… The Clinton Administration and many in Congress maintained that these sanctions would deprive Iran of the ability to acquire weapons of mass destruction (WMD) and to fund terrorist groups by hindering its ability to modernize its key petroleum sector.'[198]

Iran's 60 major oil fields are mostly old, with some being depleted altogether. From 1979 until 1997 no major investment was made in Iran's oil industry. A study in 1998 concluded that, out of the 60 oil fields, 57 of them need major technical studies, repairs, upgrading, and pressurizing, which would require at least 145 billion dollars in investments in the country's oil industry within a ten-year period.[199] As a result of ILSA, many international companies reduced or terminated their investments in the Iranian energy sector, including those that could have helped Iran address its domestic refinery problems.[200] In addition, the sanctions prevented Iran from partnering with the US LNG plant manufacturers. It should be noted that there has never been an LNG plant built without any US component. This means higher end-prices for natural gas for Iran.[201]

It must also be kept in mind that some foreign oil companies were working in Iran's oil industry, but, due to sanctions and high risk, have frozen plans to invest billions of dollars in several projects.

## 3.2.4.
### IRAN'S NUCLEAR PROGRAM

Although the government of Iran emphasizes that its nuclear program is peaceful and an internal issue, the international community was very concerned and insisted that Iran was planning to use it for nuclear weapons. This transformed the program into a principle aim of Iran's foreign policy and an important security issue for the UN Security Council.

In 2003, the 35-member governing board of the IAEA gave Iran an ultimatum until October 31 to prove that her nuclear program was strictly for peaceful purposes, by providing all details about the program. '…Iran's reaction was mixed: on the one hand, it reacted with indignation, calling

---

[197] Fayazmanesh 2002: 227.

[198] Katzman 2007: 1.

[199] Dubowitz 2010.

[200] Dubowitz 2010.

[201] Hafezi, Alvandi 2004.

the ultimatum 'premature' and 'unfair', while stating on the other that Iran will continue working with the IAEA.'[202]

Although there were no crippling economic sanctions and there was no oil embargo in these resolutions, Iran's energy policy was bound to the nuclear program for about one decade long (2000–2010). This is due to the fact that the nuclear program at first created high costs for the government, which could be spent on the oil and gas sectors. To illustrate, times of negative propaganda against Iran by the developed countries lead to a rise in investment costs, including insurance costs. The price of financing also goes up.[203] Second, the nuclear program increased the risk for foreign investors interested to invest in Iran's oil and gas sectors. For instance, Japan slowed down its negotiations to develop the Azaadegaan oil field (the largest field in the Middle East with estimated reserves of 26–30 billion barrels of oil) and the Shell Oil Company withdrew from negotiations to develop that same field.[204]

The sanctioned resulted in the fact that Iran's oil industry has still not recovered from damages from the Iran-Iraq war to its oil installations, electric power plants, bridges, manufacturing plants, and other elements of its infrastructure.[205] As already mentioned, Iran needs foreign investments. Moreover, to realize its full potential revenues from its oil reserves, Iran needs to carry through its stated plans of diversifying through investing in the petrochemical and profitable crude oil derivatives. Again, this requires outside investment.[206]

Iran is far behind other oil exporting countries of the Middle East in terms of developing its fossil energy resources. Iran has not even been able to increase oil production to the pre-Revolution level of 6 million barrels/day.[207] Iran is facing dwindling production problems. Based on international figures, since the fields are in the second half of their lifetime, for instance, the country lost about 200,000 barrels per day in production in 2008–2009.[208] If Iran cannot upgrade its oil facilities and industry on a timely manner, it will lose market share.

Thus, weakening of energy relations led Iran to replace Asian countries, particularly China and India, with the EU.

---

[202] Sahimi 2003.

[203] Ghaninejad 2008.

[204] Sahimi 2003.

[205] NIOC, 2008.

[206] Feiler 2010.

[207] Sahimi 2003.

[208] Sajadiyan 2009.

## 3.3.
## CONCLUSION

Iran's energy policy has changed and shifted from time to time as a result of the coalition-based decision-making process determined by the Iranian political system. The Iranian policy decision-making process allows for different political players to participate. By distributing the political power among the different political institutions, different players can push their agendas and implement them. Also, this type of structure has allowed some interest groups to intervene and participate in the country's energy policy decisions.

Among the elected and non-elected official bodies involved in Iran's energy policy, the role of the Supreme Leader is significant. By holding the highest position in the Iranian political structure, the Supreme Leader can draw up and direct the general policy of the state, which is subsequently implemented by the president and his cabinet members. Thus, the role of the Supreme Leader is also significant when analyzing Iran's energy policy developments.

On the other hand, the world's high oil and gas demand, US sanctions and the international community's reaction towards Iran's nuclear program have also shaped Iran's energy policy. To explain this impact the ability of powerful states that are able to force weaker states into compliance needs to be looked at. This can be visible in the US sanctions against Iran and its pressure on the European countries and companies to reduce trade with Iran.

It is important to keep in mind that the US pressure focused on the energy sector, including investments in Iran's oil and gas fields, rather than on the military. US also imposed restrictions on the transfer of capital and technology between Iran and the European countries. It is important that to know that in order to improve and further develop the oil industry, Iran needed foreign investments. And to do that, Iran had to re-establish contracts with the Western oil majors that could provide capital, technology and the expertise. It seems that in response to the US sanctions and following the policy of European countries, the Iranians realized that their trade needed to shift away from the West to the East Asian countries.

# 4.
# Iran- China Energy Relations

According to a European Commission's report, the 'EU was Iran's main trading partner concerning both imports and exports in 2007.' This relation was the result of the intensifying Iran - Europe dialogue that started in 2001. EU imports from Iran totaled 6.7 billion euros in 2001, whereas the value of EU exports to Iran in the same year amounted to 6.6 billion euros. Oil products represented more than 80% of EU imports from Iran.[209]

Iran's energy relations with the EU had improved because of Europe's growing demand for energy. This also led to the creation of a working group on energy at the Commission's office in Tehran in 2002, which aimed at expanding cooperation in the energy sector. According to the European Commission's report from 2003, 'better relations with Iran would guarantee a constant and stable supply of energy for the EU economy.'[210]

The EU's trade balance (counting all 25 member states) remained positive in two consecutive intervals during Khatami's government. A report published by the Embassy of the Islamic Republic of Iran in London in 2006 shows that 'more than 80% of EU's imports from Iran were energy related (mainly oil products), representing 3.9% of the EU's total imports of energy products. Iran ranked as the 6th supplier of energy products for the EU'. Finally, the Islamic Republic of Iran was the fifth major crude oil supplier to the EU in 2007 by exporting more than 12 billion euros worth of crude oil. Iran supplied 6% of the European Union's crude oil demand in 2007.[211]

Although many sanctions were imposed on Iran by the US and UN, Italy, Germany and the Netherlands were Iran's major trade partners among the EU member states in the first quarter of 2007. Based on this report published by the European Commission, quoted by the Iranian media, the volume of trade between Iran and Italy in this period amounted to 1.2 billion euros. In addition, the volume of trade with Germany and the Netherlands in the first quarter of 2007 stood at 724 million euros and 612 million euros, respectively.[212]

---

[209] European Commission 2003.

[210] European Commission 2003.

[211] NIOC 2008.

[212] Press TV 2007.

In addition, when looking at the European concerns over natural gas shortages, a study of various routes for transporting gas to Europe concluded that Qatar was too far, while Turkmenistan unable to meet the long-term needs. The study suggested Europe should woo Iran. In fact, although global hegemony was changing over the years, Europe was still eyeing Iran as the most strategic country in the region in view of its transit routes, neighborhood with countries that could affect regional balances, as well as the existence of huge gas reserves.[213]

According to the European Commission, it was expected that Western European oil imports could rise from 55% of the then current consumption to 65% in 2010 and possibly to 80% by 2020.[214] But according to Iran's Press News on June 19, 2007, trade data in 2007 indicated a 6% decline compared to the figures of 2006. In addition, investment in Iran's hydrocarbon sector had declined sharply since 2004.[215] Even though there was growth potential in those years, Iran's trade and the country's development was severely harmed by the ongoing problems caused by the US sanctions and the Iranian nuclear program.

Thus, with the increasing US sanctions on Iran's energy sector and the declining Iran- EU trade, Iran tried to find new energy partners. China and India with their fast-growing economies and their extensive demand for energy, reinforced Iran's inclination to further advance its economic and politically-strategic cooperation with these countries, treating them as a new market. This chapter will focus on Iran's energy relation with China.

## 4.1.
## IRAN'S ENERGY POLICY AND ASIAN COUNTRIES

Iran's energy relations with Asian countries has been an opportunity due to the region's high demand for oil and gas. According to energy statistics, 'Asia's oil consumption will increase from 1.07 billion tons (22 million barrels per day) in 2005 to 2.05 billion tons (43 million barrels per day) in 2030, an increase of 2.6% per annum.'[216] In addition, according to the International Energy Organization, developing Asia (Asia minus Japan and South Korea) will increase its demand for energy by more than 42% in 2030, compared to a 26% increase in the demand of the United States and Canada. The impressive growth of energy consumption in Asia accounts

---

[213] Maleki 2007.

[214] Payvand's Iran News 2008.

[215] Press TV 2007.

[216] Toichi 2008.

for its large share in the increase of the global energy consumption. In Asia's industrializing countries, the average annual energy consumption growth settles at 3%, with the at 1.7% worldwide.[217]

The two Asian giants, i.e. China and India, both have rapidly growing economies. The World Bank says India will become the third largest economy after China and the US by 2025.[218] Thus, while Iran needs the Asian consumers, the Asian countries also are engaged in a frantic search of energy suppliers to sustain their economic growth. Iran's oil and gas resources, and also its specific geography, has given it an important role to play on the Asian oil markets. In addition, Iran's geographic location gives it the ability to transfer its energy resources from the south, east and north of the country to the Asian consumers through pipelines. However, Iran has to consider elements, such as political issues, that can be obstacles to its role on the Asian oil markets.

## 4.2.
## IRAN-CHINA ENERGY RELATIONS

Prior to the Iranian revolution, the last Chinese official to meet with the late Shah Mohammed Reza Pahlavi was Chinese Communist Party chief Hua Kuo-feng. The meeting did not appeal to the Iranian masses. Concerned about the dicey nature of China-Iran relations, the political leadership in China immediately recognized the new government, expressing its feelings to pursue friendly relations. The onset of the Iran-Iraq War in September 1980 forced China into a delicate balancing act.[219] It considered both countries to be allies and tried not to take sides, urging a peaceful resolution of the conflict. It also welcomed Iran's condemnation of the Soviet invasion of Afghanistan and encouraged Iran to mend its relations with the US. As Washington attempted to punish the Iranian government for allowing militant students to take its embassy personnel hostage, the Chinese leadership displayed its willingness to part ways with the US in order to maintain its relations with Iran.[220]

Like the former Soviet Union, in 1980, the Chinese government refused to support the UN arms embargo against Iran under Security Council Resolution 598. The Chinese government also abstained from voting on a US sponsored resolution to impose economic sanctions on Iran. Ali Khamenei, as president

---

[217] *International Energy Outlook* 2009.

[218] Blank 2007.

[219] Dorraj, Currier 2008.

[220] Dorraj, Currier 2008.

of Iran, visited China and assured Deng Xiaoping of Iran's commitment to expand friendly relations between the two nations. As a result of this closer relationship, Sino-Iranian trade increased substantially in the 1980s. Total trade between the two countries increased from $627 million to $1.627 billion.[221]

The end of the Iran-Iraq War in 1988 provided China with a new opportunity to participate in a much needed economic reconstruction effort in Iran and emerge as the provider of arms and technology to Iran. The strained Iranian relations with the US and Western Europe rendered Iran an alluring market for China. This was the period when China's economy began to grow rapidly, exponentially increasing China's need for new sources of energy and investment markets. Iran needed a reliable buyer for its oil and gas, and a supplier of military equipment and weapon systems. This made the rationale behind the mutually beneficial relationship between the two even more patently clear.[222]

Although the relations were first limited to military purchases by Iran, this soon extended to vast economic exchanges. State-oriented economies, cheap Chinese commodities, easy economic and banking systems and exchanges were among the factors that gradually enhanced the two countries' economic relations.[223] This soon led to China's further involvement in Iran's infrastructure related activities, such as roads, railways and urban construction, as well as oil and gas infrastructure. These plans required a long-term Chinese presence in the country. Over the last decade, China's involvement has slowly won Iran's confidence both in economic and politically-strategic activities.[224]

## 4.2.1.
### IRAN'S OIL EXPORTS TO CHINA

In 1995, the Iranian News Agency announced that the country would expand production to 60,000 bpd.[225] In the same year, in order to expand oil exports to China and enable China to refine the imported crude faster, Iran agreed to invest $25 million in China's oil-refining industry.[226] In 1997, China pledged to expand the imports of Iranian oil from 70,000 bpd to 100,000 bpd in 1999 and to 270,000 bpd in 2000.[227]

---

[221] Huwaidin 2002.

[222] Dorraj, Currier 2008.

[223] Barzegar 2008.

[224] Barzegar 2008.

[225] Dorraj, Currier 2008.

[226] Jin 2005.

[227] Jin 2005.

By 2002, Iran was responsible for more than 15% of the PRC's annual oil imports.[228] By 2003, China became the second largest consumer of oil in the world. In 2005, Iran was the second-largest provider, after Saudi Arabia, of oil to China; the two countries have signed oil and gas contracts worth $70 billion.[229] It should be kept in mind that while Chinese exports to Iran were very diverse, ranging from electronics and machinery to arms, consumer goods and textiles, oil accounts for 80% of Chinese imports from Iran.[230] And, 'in January 2006, Iran replaced Saudi Arabia as China's number one source of imported oil.'[231] China imported 3.6 million bp/d of crude oil in 2008, of which approximately 1.8 million bpd (50%) came from the Middle East, 1.1 million bpd (30%) from Africa, 101,000 bpd (3%) from the Asia-Pacific region, and 603,000 bpd (17%) came from other countries.[232] The rising demand for oil in China and Iran's vast reserves pushed energy towards the center of the countries' bilateral relationship.

### 4.2.2.
IRAN-CHINA COOPERATION IN ENERGY

As mentioned earlier, in 1996, the Clinton administration's Iran-Libya Sanctions Act (ILSA) imposed tough penalties on foreign companies and individuals found to be investing more than $20 million in oil and gas development in Iran.[233] This initiative further hampered Iran's ability to modernize and expand its production capabilities. This proved to be a boon for China. While the West European oil companies began to object to the 'extraterritoriality' of US sanctions and defied them, China gained confidence that, despite intense anti-Chinese sentiment in the US Congress, Washington could not single out China for punitive action.[234] Iran's need of investors to explore its vast oil reserves and rebuild its war-torn and decrepit oil infrastructure meant that China offered to rebuild the facilities and engage in joint-venture exploration and development of new oil and gas fields.[235] In addition, China hoped to lock into the Iranian oil market for the long haul. After allaying Iranian fears about Chinese technological

---

[228] Jin 2005.

[229] Jin 2005.

[230] Dorraj, Currier 2008.

[231] Energy Information Administration, China 2009.

[232] Energy Information Administration, China 2009.

[233] Clawson 2010.

[234] Dorraj, Currier 2008.

[235] Dorraj, Currier 2008.

capabilities, the two countries signed an agreement in 1997 for cooperation in prospecting and exploration.[236]

Consequently, according to Manochehr Dorraj and Carrie L. Currier '...China cited the 1999 signing by Royal Dutch Shell of a deal with Iran worth $850 million to rebuild Iranian oil fields damaged during the Iran-Iraq War to justify its own investment in Iranian oil and gas fields.'[237]

This led to a discovery of vast reserves in the Azadegan oil field in 1999 (estimated to have 26 billion barrels of oil, making it one of the largest undeveloped oil reserves in the world, worth $2.6 billion).[238] This encouraged the Iranian government to think about the Asian allies. However, in 2000, President Khatami decided to grant the development rights to a Japanese firm, but, in order to prevent a rift with China, the National Iranian oil Company (NIOC) granted the China National Petroleum Corporation (CNPC) an $85 million contract to drill 19 wells in its existing natural gas fields in southern Iran. This was followed by a $13 million oil contract between the two in 2001.[239]

In August 2000, CNPC won its first drilling contract in Iran (to drill 19 gas wells in southern Iran). The most significant breakthrough in this area is the widely reported preliminary agreement (reached in October 2004) between the National Iranian Oil Company (NIOC) and Sinopec to develop the Yadavaran oil field, whereby the NIOC would sell 150,000 bpd of crude oil to China at market prices over a period of 25 years once the field becomes fully operational.[240]

In March 2004, the state-owned Zhuhai Zhenrong Corporation (a spin-off of NORINCO) agreed to import 110 million tons of Iranian liquefied natural gas (LNG) over 25 years, a deal worth approximately $20 billion.[241] According to the terms of the Yadavaran project's agreement, Sinopec committed itself to purchase 10 million tons per year of liquefied natural gas (LNG) over a period of 25 years, beginning in 2009.[242] A few months later, Sinopec and NIOC signed another contract that would allow China to buy Iranian LNG for the next 30 years.[243] This deal was estimated to

---

[236] Dorraj, Currier 2008.

[237] Dorraj, Currier 2008.

[238] Dorraj, Currier 2008: 269.

[239] Dorraj, Currier 2008: 269.

[240] Islamic Republic News Agency 2004.

[241] Calabrese 2006.

[242] Calabrese 2006.

[243] Garver 2006: 271.

be worth \$70–100 billion.[244] In addition, CNPC was also given the right to invest in the exploration of the Yadavaran oil field in exchange for the right to purchase 150,000 bpd at market prices, once the oil field became operational.[245] Also, another area of cooperation would be the process of upgrading Iranian refineries and strengthening of the oil recovery. CNPC is engaged in an oil recovery and extraction projects to increase the production of Iran's Masjed Soleiman field based on a buy-back contract. Iran and China also signed a preliminary agreement to construct a gas condensate refinery in Bandar Abbas, aimed at raising the production of gasoline, which currently constitutes 56% of the refinery's output.[246]

In June 2005, CNPC won a bid to develop the Khoudasht oil block in western Iran.[247] In addition, Sinopec expressed interest in taking up the Azadegan exploration and development project. According to Sinopec's officials, in 2004, the U.S. embassy in Beijing requested that Sinopec withdraw its bid, but Sinopec refused.[248]

In April 2006, the Islamic Republic of Iran Shipping Lines (IRISL) awarded an estimated \$180 million contract to Sino-Pacific Heavy Industries to build six 53,000 deadweight tonnage(dwt) carriers (with the option of building four more) at the latter's Dayang shipyard in Yangzhou.[249] However, the National Iranian Oil Tanker Company (NITC) planned to order another 35 vessels to be built by 2010, including 10 liquefied natural gas carriers, a more complex ship that costs almost twice as much as crude-oil tankers.[250] NITC Planning Manager Abdol-Samad Taagol gave some indication of the role that Chinese companies might play in this effort when he said that 'we'll give priority to Chinese shipyards if China is to become our biggest consumer of gas,' though added that Iran had made 'no firm commitment yet.'[251]

China has also become an active participant in Iran's development of Caspian Sea oil and gas and the modernization of its facilities in Neka and other regions. The Neka-Sari pipeline, built by a consortium of Chinese companies led by Sinopec and CNPC (completed in 2003) carries Russian crude oil shipped from the Caspian ports of Astrakhan and Volgagrad from the Iranian port of

[244] Garver 2006: 271.

[245] Garver 2006: 271.

[246] Marketos 2009.

[247] Dorraj, Currier 2008.

[248] Dorraj, Currier 2008.

[249] Calabrese 2006.

[250] Calabrese 2006

[251] Calabrese 2006

Neka farther into Iran.[252] Another pipeline being built with Chinese participation will carry oil from the Neka terminal to a refinery on the southern outskirts of Tehran in the municipality of Ray. In addition, China is sympathetic to Iran's attempt to bring Caspian oil and gas through pipelines to the southern Iranian ports for shipping to Europe and Asia. The United States is opposed to this initiative, which will expand Iran's economic and strategic clout.[253] China, however, remains undeterred so far by the negative US reactions to its attempts to forge closer relations with the Islamic Republic. China's aggressive cultivation of the Iranian market has been fruitful. China now supplants Germany and other European powers, which until 2006 were Iran's largest trade partners. In 2007, Iran-China trade volume increased by 27% and reached $15 billion.[254]

During these years, China and Iran worked separately and jointly to augment their capacity to handle the increased volumes of oil, gas, and refined products moving from the Persian Gulf to East Asia. For example, in order to support the growth of LNG imports from Iran and other suppliers, China was building receiving terminals at Guangdong, Shanghai, and Fujian. Meanwhile, China's main shipbuilding enterprises won contracts to supply Iran with oil tankers.[255] However, China imports a large quantity of oil and intends to import significant amounts of LNG from Iran. The two major projects of North Pars gas field exploration and Yadavaran oil field development are among the most important projects between the two countries. A deal involving the development of the North Pars gas field between CNOOC and National Iran Oil Company (NIOC) was signed. The project involved an investment of $16 billion from the Chinese side.[256] It was also 2007 when the Yadavaran project between Sinopec and NIOC was finalized. Sinopec has to develop it and buy 10 mn tons of LNG over 25 years.[257] Chinese activities in Iran include refinery upgrades, as well as pipeline and engineering services, such as drilling. The main rationale for cooperating with Iran is not only to secure the supply of oil and gas, but also to seek commercial opportunities for Chinese NOCs, as Iran is one of the few countries in the Middle East that assigns China the right to conduct business in its upstream sector. China was the largest petroleum trade partner of Iran in 2007, and is one of the few countries to break US sanctions against Iran, which 'penalizes foreign companies for investing more than $20 million.'[258] Therefore,

---

[252] Dorraj, Currier 2008.

[253] Dorraj, Currier 2008.

[254] Calabrese 2006.

[255] Calabrese 2006.

[256] Ma 2008.

[257] Ma 2008.

[258] Ma 2008.

China is also critically important for Iran in terms of commercial and political support on the international arena.

At multilateral relations, Iran's geographic situation gives it the ability to transfer its energy resources from the south, east and north of the country to Asian consumers through pipelines. This is especially true in the gas sector. As mentioned before, Iran has the second largest natural gas reserves in the world, and gas has become a priority in the energy security strategies of central and east Asian consumers. This provides the country with strategic leverage in defining the world's hydrocarbon regime. In this situation, Iran wanted energy cooperation with China in Central Asia and West Asian countries.[259] It seems that the Iranian government has not been successful achieving this aim though.

## 4.3.
## IRAN'S POLITICAL STRATEGY IN ENERGY RELATIONS WITH CHINA

Iran's energy relations with China do derive its subsistence also provides political support, especially in context of US policy. With the United States trying to isolate Iran, Iran needs the support of regional power countries, such as China. Iran's nuclear program has been a topic at the United Nations and, specifically, the United Nations Security Council (UNSC) at many sessions. It has been addressed in several ways in numerous Security Council resolutions. The five permanent members of the UN Security Council, Britain, China, France, Russia and the US, and Germany singed some resolutions against Iran's nuclear program. So, Iran was trying to strengthen its relation with China in order to use its role in United Nations Security Council. According to the Iranian strategy, China, was not going to risk its economic interests in relations with Iran by supporting United Nations Security Council sanctions against Iran. According to Phillip Gordon, a senior fellow for US Foreign Policy at the Brookings Institution;

'...Beijing is reluctant to pursue hard-line economic sanctions due to the Chinese Communist Party's (CCP's) priorities of maintaining power and social stability. In order to maintain social stability, China needs consistent economic development and for economic development, China needs massive amounts of affordable energy to fuel its booming economy. Thus, China is reluctant to do anything that would interfere with its energy relationship with Iran....'[260]

---

[259] Vaezi 2006.

[260] Gordon 2007: 17–18.

China's policy towards Iran is, therefore, complicated because of its role on the global market. It is affected by new world politics.

## 4.4.
## CHINA'S ENERGY POLICY TOWARDS IRAN

Although Deng Xiaoping is known as the architect of modern China, the role of Chou En-lai, China's PM during Mao Zedong's rule, was more important.[261] He believed that China had to be powerful and the country's differences on the international scene had to be reduced from the security to the political level.[262] According to En-lai strategy '...the policy of peace and neutrality of the nationalist countries must be respected and no country must consider China as a security threat.'[263] Meanwhile, Chou En-lai was the initiator of China's developments that aimed to alter China-West ties and change the West's negative attitude towards China.[264] Following this policy of Chou En-lai, after Mao's death, Deng Xiaoping, as the country's new leader, gradually could transform the economy of China from the ideological base of 'socialism's struggle against capitalism' to a 'socialist market economy'. This change manifested itself in the economy, when the country's gross domestic product (GDP) grew by an average of 9.7% in 1982–1992.[265]

The aim of the Chinese was to become a key global player. To achieve this, China needed both economic and military instruments in diplomacy. What is more, this goal would not be possible to reach without development of China's foreign relations. The collapse of the Soviet Union and the ensuing changes in global politics after the Cold War offered China the right conditions. China's government too began developing its foreign policy agendas, which seemed to be closer in tune to the international relations theory of complex interdependence, in order to lead towards cooperation on all fronts with other nations. Thus, the old diplomacy that had long avoided most international affairs began to be ignored and the country became more willing to share the responsibilities that come with the great-power status.

This new policy pushed China into the global marketplace and strategically created a country that was interdependent with the rest of the economies of the WTO, particularly the United States.[266] As a result of its WTO

---

[261] Sariolghalam 2007.

[262] Sariolghalam 2007.

[263] Ministry of Foreign Affairs 2010.

[264] Yan 2006.

[265] Ong 2004.

[266] Brenner 2001.

membership, according to US customs statistics in 2002, China exported $125.2 billion, or 38.5% of total Chinese exports, to the United States (including those transshipped through Hong Kong), making the United States China's largest export market.[267] The two-way trade between China and the US has grown from $33 billion in 1992 to $147.3 billion in 2002.[268]

Although China's development was significant as a result of its new foreign relations in 2000, but, still, to become powerful, it needed to develop military and economic pillars. This is because '...Chinese do not have long-term military capacity and their military strategy is based on deterrence, they do not have military moves and technological power in this field either. There is just a small local industry and for the rest they are significantly dependent on Russia....'[269]

Therefore, the Chinese have been seeking co-operation with the US and EU to develop their economy and employ military technology. It can be easily seen that the Chinese economy became dependent on Western countries and the US. Meanwhile, China's dependence on the US and the Western consumer market has shifted its foreign policies in some area of its conflicts with the US. Iran could be one area of conflict due to China's economic liberalization policy that has increased its demand for additional sources of energy.[270]

## 4.4.1.
### CHINA'S ENERGY DEMAND AND INTERDEPENDENCE

When the anticipated petroleum reserves in Xinjiang province and in the East and South China Seas failed to meet expectations and with the Daqing field's reserves running down, China's energy production, particularly its domestic oil production, failed to keep up the pace and China became a net importer of crude oil in 1993. [271]China's demand for imported oil increased fast from 1993 to 2002 and its oil demand grew close to 90%, while domestic production grew less than 15%.[272]

By 2004, with the economy still growing at 9.5% annually, Chinese oil demand had risen to six million barrels per day, with 40% coming from

---

[267] Tung 2002: 2

[268] Sariolghalam 2007.

[269] Sariolghalam 2007.

[270] See: Ziegler 2006: 1–23.

[271] Leverett, Leverett 2009.

[272] Leverett, Leverett 2009.

imports.[273] According to the *Oil & Gas Journal (OGJ)*, China had 18.3 billion barrels of proven oil reserves and was producing 3.8 million barrels per day (Mmbbl/d) of oil in 2006,[274] but its oil demand continued to increase and grow from 6.98 mln (bpd) in 2006 to 7.59 mln (bpd) in 2007. It rose to 8.05 mln (bpd) in 2008.[275] At present, China is the second largest consumer of energy and the second consumer of oil and gas in Asia.[276] '…Given the country's booming economy, oil products' demand is projected to increase by 5.6% per year on average to almost 10 million bpd by 2012, consolidating its position as the second largest oil consumer after the US.'[277]

The growing demand of China for energy and the necessity of importing it have made energy security a vital issue for the country. This matter has become a priority on China's foreign policy agenda. As Robert Kaplan mentioned '… China's insatiable demand for energy and natural resources is driving its strategic policy, as it expands its military reach and influence both on continental as well as in maritime Asia.'[278] This caused China to depend on the world's energy market, strengthening its relations with the oil and gas exporter countries.

Moreover, China's dependence on foreign oil and gas resources forces it to be involved in political issues. As already mentioned, although the African countries also contribute a significant amount to China's oil imports, according to FACTS Global Energy, the Middle East is China's main oil reserve. According to the reports, China imported 3.6 million bbl/d of crude oil in 2008, of which approximately 1.8 million bbl/d (50%) came from the Middle East, 1.1 million bbl/d (30%) from Africa, 101,000 bbl/d (3%) from the Asia-Pacific region, and 603,000 bbl/d (17%) came from other countries.[279] Meanwhile, given the general decline in energy production, particularly oil production, in other parts of the world, the Middle East, especially the Persian Gulf, is the most important region that can provide reliable energy to the world's consumers in the next 50 years.[280]

And although the new Chinese foreign policy is based on avoiding conflict with other countries, its energy security is a significant challenge that requires it to be linked to the Middle East and, especially, the Persian Gulf region. Therefore, China, like many other countries, is becoming more de-

---

[273] Leverett, Bader 2005: 189.

[274] Energy Information Administration, China 2006.

[275] Energy Information Administration, China 2009.

[276] Energy Information Administration, China 2009.

[277] Energy Information Administration, China 2009.

[278] Blumenthal 2010.

[279] Energy Information Administration, China 2009.

[280] Jaffe 2002: 115–133.

pendent on oil imports from this crisis-ridden region. For instance, among the Persian Gulf countries, Iran is the second oil supplier of China. But because of its conflict with the US, this has also affected China's relations with other countries. This is because the West and especially the United States are sticking to their isolation policy towards Iran through diplomatic and economic channels, international pressure and cross-societal exchanges.

## 4.4.2.
### CHINESE ENERGY SECURITY AND IRAN

'…During the Cold War, China was the only major country that stood at the intersection of the two superpower camps, a target of influence and enmity for both.'[281] China also regarded itself as a leader of the Third World and political supporter of the developing countries and anti-West.[282] Following this approach, China's relations with Iran strengthened tremendously with Iran's shift in its international political and economic relations spurred by the 1979 Islamic revolution.

The Islamic government's foreign policy became ideological and idealist. It acquired a profile, which was hostile towards the West, particularly the United States. This caused a complete transformation of Iran's bilateral and multilateral relations. Iran's economic policy became more nationalistic, especially in the energy sector.

As already mentioned, this led to the cancellation of all oil agreements with the Western states and companies, and a change in rules on foreign investment, and agreements with foreign countries and companies. In these circumstances, Beijing viewed Iran's Islamic Republic as a potential political ally and sought to cultivate a strategic partnership with Tehran. This was also because Iran was an important regional power, capable of playing a leading role in the diplomatic balance in the Persian Gulf and Middle East, hence a highly valuable anti-Western partner for China.

In the meantime, the Iran-Iraq war increased Iran's demand for arms and weapons. Thus, the '…Chinese adopted an 'arms for oil' formula, providing weapons in exchange for oil from Iran.'[283] This policy provided oil resources for China and also transferred arms and weapon technology to Iran. The deals gave China billions of dollars and China replaced Western countries as the weapons' provider.[284] For example, in 1978, the last year of the Shah's

---

[281] Xia 2008.

[282] Junbo 2010.

[283] Chang 2008.

[284] Chang 2009.

rule in Iran, China supplied only 1% of Iran's imports – compared to 21% by the United States, 19% by Germany, 16% by Japan, and 8% by Britain. But by 1991, the United States and Britain were virtually out of the Iranian market (with 3 and less than 1%, respectively), while China's share had doubled to a still modest 2%.[285] In addition, the amount of oil exported to China from Iran in 1977 was at 300,000 tons and reached one million tons (25,000 b/d) in 1982 and two million tons (40,000 b/d) by 1989–1990.[286] This trade made China develop a relationship with Iran for the next decade.

## 4.4.3.
### CHINA-IRAN AND INTERDEPENDENCE

In the 1990s, when the US intervened in Iraq's invasion of Kuwait, trying to prove regional dominance, it was also the time of the collapse of the Soviet Union. These events forced Beijing to set out a new foreign policy and speed up the development of its 'socialist market economy.'[287] As already mentioned earlier, the Chinese needed natural resources to develop their 'socialist market economy'. They needed a guaranteed route to supply their energy. China, therefore, sought trade agreements, oil and gas contracts, scientific and technological cooperation, and even multilateral security arrangements with countries in the Middle East.[288] This changed its relations with Iran, the world's fourth biggest oil producer.

As mentioned earlier, China-Iran relations developed especially after the US imposed tough sanctions on Iran's energy sector in 1996.[289] The sanctions limited Iran's ability to develop its oil industry, but created an opportunity for China.[290] China was pursuing a strategy of dominating the Iranian oil market. In 1997, China pledged to expand imports of Iranian oil from 70,000 b, d to 100,000 b/d in 1999 and to 270,000 b/d in 2000.[291] But, getting the energy from Iran had pushed China to support Iran politically and particularly in the United Nations in 1990s. Iran's nuclear program was an issue discussed at the United Nations and, specifically, the United Nations Security Council (UNSC) at many sessions and Beijing was reluctant to pursue hardline economic sanctions by the United Nations towards Iran.

---

[285] See: Garver 2006.

[286] Dorraj 2008.

[287] Junbo 2010.

[288] Dumbaugh 2005.

[289] Franssen, Morton 2002.

[290] Dorraj 2008.

[291] Dorraj 2008.

However, '…China needed consistent economic development and for that, China requested massive amounts of affordable energy to fuel its booming economy. Thus, China was reluctant to do anything that would interfere with its energy relationship with Iran.'[292] Also, in January 2007, China's foreign ministry spokesman, Liu Jianchao, said the 'US should not interfere in China's relations with Iran. China called for flexibility and patience in negotiating the issue. China insists that sanctions should only aim at nuclear trade, not general commerce, arms sales or investment in energy projects and other sectors of Iran's economy.'[293] Thus, Iran received some political support from China, but it seems that China does not support Iran if it affects its relations with the US.

China many times refused to vote for economic sanctions against Iran's nuclear program, fearing interruption to the flow of energy supplies, which are essential for China's booming economy.

Some believe that the Sino-Iranian cooperation on arms was not only confined to conventional weapons. According to McLaughlin,[294] '…from 1984 to 1997, China provided considerable aid to Iran's fledgling nuclear program. This assistance included training Iranian scientists, helping to construct facilities, direct hardware sales and military aid.' Meanwhile, according to Western sources, '…as early as 1997 Iran had received from China's Great Wall Industries Corporation, guidance, and solid propellant motor technology, as well as general missile testing technology.'[295] Thus, Iran also was the best market weapon for China.

Consequently, in the 1990s, China could meet some of the strategic needs of Iran in issues related to development and security, while Iran could manage its strategic concerns about energy security. It seems that there was a mutual willingness on the part of both China and Iran to use energy as an opportunity in their relations. This relationship was going to increase their interdependence due to their abilities to provide for at least one of the strategic needs of each country in case China's policy failed to get closer to the West.

4.5.
SINO-US ECONOMIC INTERDEPENDENCE AND IRAN

China's policy towards Iran started to change in the 2000s with Beijing deciding to expand its participation in international organizations. This changed its relations with the United States and the rest of the world.

---

[292] Gordon 2007.

[293] Wellman, Frasco 2011.

[294] McLaughlin 2006.

[295] Federation of American Scientists 2008.

**Sino-US Relations:**

China and the United States, until the end of the Cold War, played all politics as a strategic measure against each other. However, the end of the Cold War and the resulting changes on the international scene pushed China's and US relationship into a new territory. China became a member of WTO in 2001. '... China appeared willing to embrace many norms and rules of the global economic system of which the United States was the chief architect and dominant player.'[296] This helped China connect to the world economy and, particularly the economy of the United States and Western countries. This connection has increased Chinese economic interdependence with the US.

Despite the growing economic interdependence between the two countries increased, there are still areas of contention between them. Some conflict are linked to China's economic growth. But, due to China's dependence on the world economy, the US has become more inclined to use diplomacy and economic instruments in its dealings with China rather than military aggression or the threat of aggression in order to solve its regional and global disputes with the Chinese.[297] Therefore, as Brenner has pointed out, '...each of these areas are continually being resurfaced and mutually linked to one another in multilateral discussions and agreements, bilateral, government-level talks, and increased societal exchanges.'[298]

The global oil market can be considered one of the areas of conflict between the US and China due to the fact that '...the United States' strategy is based on ensuring oil flows, especially the oil of the Middle Eastern countries to the United States and its partners.' Therefore, the United States has established firm control over the Persian Gulf region militarily through two wars with Iraq. The Americans also have directly interfered with China's role in the regional oil and gas markets in the Persian Gulf. A conflict has arisen over the sales of dual-use technologies and equipment. From the US perspective, China's military cooperation and trade of dual-use items with Iran, Iraq, Syria and Saudi Arabia amounts to a weapons-for-oil strategy.[299] For instance, in December 2003, the American Embassy in Beijing pressured CNPC into retracting its bid for the exploration of 16 new oil fields in Iran.[300]

Although the US has pressured China because of its energy relations with Iran, this has so far failed to become a source of conflict between the two countries because China has showed that it was not going to harm

---

[296] Dumbaugh 2008.

[297] Brenner 2001.

[298] Brenner 2001.

[299] Daojiong 2006: 12.

[300] Daojiong 2006: 12.

its relations with the United States to strengthen its ties with Iran. China finds itself in an uncomfortable position in catering to the political and economic needs of some of its suppliers there. The effects and the reasons behind this policy of China towards Iran are reviewed in two sections.

### Importance of Iran's oil for China:

China's oil and gas imports from Iran increased gradually from 270,000 b/d in 2000 to 450,000 barrels per day in 2007.[301] The increase was the result of many agreements in the oil and gas sectors, which were signed between the two countries in absence of the Western countries and companies. For instance, some Chinese companies partners up with Iran on two important projects: the North Pars gas field exploration deal and Yadavaran oil field development project. The deal between CNOOC and National Iran Oil Company (NIOC) involved the development of the North Pars gas field.[302] The project involved an investment of $16 billion from the Chinese side. The Yadavaran deal, between Sinopec and NIOC, was worth $2 billion. According to the deal, Sinopec has to develop it and buy 10 million tons of LNG gas over 25 years.[303] These deals made China the largest petroleum trade partner of Iran in 2007. China replaced Germany and other European powers, which until 2006 were Iran's largest trade partners. In 2007, the volume of Iran-China trade rose 27% to reach $15 billion.[304]

China improved its energy relations with Iran through bilateral agreements and emerged as one of the few countries to break US sanctions against Iran, which penalizes foreign companies for investing more than $20 million. But Beijing did not successfully pursue this policy related to some multilateral projects due to US pressure. For instance, China was sympathetic to Iran's attempt to bring Caspian oil and gas through pipelines to the southern Iranian ports for shipping to Europe and Asia. The United States was adamantly opposed to this initiative, which will expand Iran's economic and strategic clout.[305] As mentioned above, China's new policy is based on avoiding conflict with the US. Thus, in its investment in and transit of energy from Central Asia, it has tried to find ways that do not cause conflict with the US.[306] Continuing this policy, in December 2005, the Atasu-Alashankou oil pipeline from Kazakhstan to China was

---

[301] Energy Information Administration, China 2008.

[302] Calabrese 2006.

[303] Dorraj 2008.

[304] Kemenade 2009: 112.

[305] Dorraj 2008.

[306] Chan 2001.

inaugurated.[307] In addition to that, during the first half of 2006, China announced its plans to construct a natural gas pipeline from Kazakhstan to China, which would run parallel to its Atasu-Alashankou oil pipeline.[308]

In addition, China proposed prospective gas pipelines with Uzbekistan and Turkmenistan that would link up with the projected gas pipeline. Such a pipeline would not only transport Kazakh gas to China, but would also connect with the Turkmen and Uzbek gas pipeline.[309] In both Uzbekistan and Turkmenistan, China also become engaged in efforts to discuss funding of energy exploration. China intended to import Turkmen gas from Tajikistan through a pipeline.[310] China focused on these projects even though Beijing considered Iran as the best way to transit oil and gas from Central Asia, but cancelled such projects due to its relations with the US.

### China's political support and partnership with Iran:

Based on China's new policy in the new world order, the country needs to cast its net in international relations as wide as possible in order to become a genuine global power. As a result, China has avoided permanence of its political support for Iran. China-Iran relations were still looked at by China through the context of the US isolation policy towards Iran. John Garver describes it as China's 'Persian Gulf dilemma.'[311] According to Garver '...this 'dilemma' requires China to balance a major interest in maintaining its commitment to the United States against its interests in building ties with the important (Persian) Gulf countries, such as the Islamic Republic.'[312] It seems that China's leaders have been careful not to let their country's developing ties to Iran be perceived in Washington as a direct challenge to America's longstanding hegemonic position in the (Persian) Gulf.[313]

Meanwhile, according to Jean-François Seznec '...political instability and even the threat of US or Israeli military retaliation against an Iranian provocation have made Iran a less than attractive partner for Beijing.'[314] Chinese leaders have learned that Iran is a hard place to do business. This is reflected in the decreasing trade flows between Iran and China, with the total bilateral trade amounting to $21 billion, including $10 billion in oil

---

[307] Energy Information Administration, China 2008.

[308] Blank 2006.

[309] Blank 2006.

[310] Blank 2006.

[311] Leverett, Leverett 2009.

[312] Leverett, Leverett 2009.

[313] Leverett, Leverett 2009.

[314] Wakefield, Hathaway 2010.

trade. By contrast, China's total trade with Saudi Arabia amounts to $60 billion, which includes 20% of China's oil supply.[315]

Moreover, although Iran is a market for China's weapons, the Chinese are more interested in the consumption markets of the US and Europe. The United States with its 300 million-strong population and the EU with its 500 milion citizens are attractive markets.[316] It has to be kept in mind that the American and European markets are a priority for every producer. China needs America's market, its industry and technology, and optimally utilizes the stable economic norms of the international system.

Consequently, China has strengthened its ties with the West by voting on Iran's sanctions. China supported some of the United Nations Security Council (UNSC) resolutions against Iran's nuclear enrichment program. Like Russia, China abstained from voting in the IAEA Board of Governors in 2005 and voted in favor of sending the issue to the UNSC in 2006. In addition to that, like Russia, China voted for United Nations Security Council Resolution (UNSCR) 1696, as well as all of the sanctions resolutions. It also voted for UNSCR 1835, while expressing the desire that the resolution would not lead to more sanctions against Iran.[317]

As a result, China has been unwilling to risk conflicts with the US or other Western countries due to its relations with Iran. It seems that Beijing has let Moscow take the lead in opposing or watering down anti-Iran sanctions proposed by the United States and its European partners. This is the reason why Europe and America have never faced China's serious opposition. As a matter of fact, they have never had major problems with China on Iran. As mentioned earlier, this was reflected in China's new foreign policy that was characterized by its economic interdependence with the West, which is closer in line with the complex interdependence theory.

4.6.
CONCLUSION

Although China has continued to build energy ties with Iran, it is important to realize that the current government of China has been developed its foreign policy agendas that are closer in line with the complex interdependence than the realist theory. The new policy has pushed China to develop closer relationships with the Western countries and particularly the United States. This policy has been welcomed by the US, which means

[315] Wakefield, Hathaway 2010.

[316] Sariolghalam 2007.

[317] Richardson 2008.

that relations between the two are progressing, at least in areas of economic cooperation and interdependence.

Growth in economic interdependence has limited China's foreign policy power on the international scene. This is because the Chinese lack the ability to set international norms. As a matter of fact, though China is a great power, it is yet to be considered to be a global power. The Chinese have a long way to go, even as far as reaching the second-class European countries' technological and knowledge levels goes. This means that the country's economic interdependence is leading to better relations between China and the US, though there are some areas of conflict between them. The United States, in order to make China comply with its policies, is using economic linkage. As mentioned earlier, the military force is no longer used as the primary tool in international politics between the two powerful nations. Diplomacy, economic sanctions, and pressure from multilateral organizations, such as the United Nations and the WTO, are providing the means to solve many of the world's disputes. Countries no longer need to resort to violent, military means. The Chinese leaders do not want any country to perceive China as a security threat. Therefore, since, 1990 they decided not to have any political frictions with the United States.

Consequently, the new world order has caused the Chinese to agree to international sanctions against Iran over the latter's nuclear program. It is clear that its energy security policy makes China sensitive and the country may not necessarily be happy at the prospect of new sanctions against Iran, one of its major energy suppliers. But, over the last five years, Beijing was not 'on its own' in opposing new sanctions. So, as long as Washington has Moscow on board, China will not block tougher international measures against Iran. This represents a major problem for Iran because it could mean that the prospects of cooperation between the two nations are not overly rosy.

# 5.
# Iran's energy policy towards India

Iran has tried to create a strategic relationship with India based on economic interdependence. Iran's policy aims to build bilateral energy relations and alliances with India. India now becoming Iran's third biggest oil customer. This is reflected by the fact that India's External Affairs Ministry had approved of the '...Iran-India commercial relation (that) is dominated by Indian imports of Iranian crude oil, accounting for roughly 85% of Indian imports from Iran each year.'[318]

What is more, it seem that India could become the world's largest economy by 2050 after China. Taking this into account, the Iranian government argues that it lies in its interest to develop a strategic relationship with India, both politically and energy-wise.

## 5.1.
## IRAN-INDIA ENERGY COOPERATION

As reflected in the '2001 Tehran Declaration' and the '2003 New Delhi Declaration', Iran is interested in moving ahead in developing commercial and energy cooperation with India. Iran is anxious to get its hydrocarbons out of the ground and onto new markets, making the energy-hungry India a good partner.[319] Iran's crude oil exports to India ranged between 100,000 and 150,000 barrels per day (bpd), accounting for about 7.5% of India's total crude oil imports (around two million bpd) in 2005.[320] This increased to 374 thousand barrels per day in 2007[321] and reached 426,360 barrels per day in 2009.[322]

Moreover, Iran has tried to export gas to India by signing an agreement with India on the Iran-Pakistan-India gas pipeline. It is clear that Iran is interested in India's gas consumption, but this agreement can also be considered as a regional project and a multilateral agreement. Although '… in the rapidly intensifying international energy game, Iran holds a master

---

[318] Kronstadt, Katzman 2006: 5.

[319] Fair 2007.

[320] Fair 2007.

[321] Energy Information Administration, Iran 2007.

[322] Reuters 2009.

key to the most staggering roadblock to India's economic growth – energy insecurity,'[323] there are some elements which have impacted on Iran-India multilateral energy relations. For instance, there are two main challenges in bringing Iran- Pakistan- India project to fruition.

'...The first challenge is the historic conflict between India and Pakistan, and the second and more important challenge lies in the American perception that most other Western countries seem to agree with – that Iran should not be allowed to make long-term commitments on its strategic resources with non-Western countries.'[324]

As such, many issues, such as India-US relations, the US-Iran conflict, and India-Pakistan differences, have affected and effectively delayed the project.

Iran's attempts to cooperate on energy issues with India in Central Asia can also be viewed as an example of this delicate balancing act. It seems that due to challenges faced by the massive pipeline (Iran-Pakistan-India), India needs to import gas from the central Asian countries. It also competes with China for oil and gas resources in other regions. China had, for example, reached out to Myanmar before India did and booked all the gas Myanmar had to offer.[325] This means that India's energy demand from Central Asia is now bigger.

However, the question that arises is how India could gain access to Central Asia's oil and gas resources. Pipelines from Central Asia to India via Afghanistan and Pakistan would be the first possibility, but it has two disadvantages. First, each of these pipelines would cost $8 billion.[326] In addition, Afghanistan is in a state of turmoil and will likely remain so for a decade or so. The historical conflict between India and Pakistan also remains an issue, making the construction of these pipelines unlikely. The Turkish route for oil from Central Asia to India via Ceyhan in Turkey, to Israel, and by tankers to India would be another option, but this seems like a non-starter as well. Transit fees and handling costs alone would make this deal expensive.[327]

India is, therefore, well aware that the best way to access central Asian oil would be through the Arabian Sea, the Iranian port of Neka in the Caspian Sea. Kazakhstan delivers oil to the Neka terminal today to further blend and swap it with Iranian oil. A pipeline already exists from Neka to Tehran and

---

[323] Afrasiabi 2008.

[324] Roshandel 1996: 627–642.

[325] McCartan 2008.

[326] Sud 2008.

[327] Sud 2008.

it has been delivering oil to the Tehran refinery for a number of years. This pipeline may be upgraded to carry Central Asian oil to the Arabian Sea.[328]

The Iranian route may therefore be the easiest and possibly the cheapest gateway for Central Asian oil and gas. Although Iran is the best way for India to access Central Asian gas resources, it seems that India has picked the Trans-Afghanistan Pipeline (TAPI) instead. The pipeline will transport Caspian Sea natural gas from Turkmenistan through Afghanistan into Pakistan and then to India. This could also be the result of India-US relations.

It seems that the India-US partnership has stopped India from pursuing multilateral energy relations with Iran and the Iran-Pakistan-India gas pipeline. According to Kaveh Afrasiabi '...the US has suggested the Turkmenistan-Afghanistan-Pakistan-India (TAPI) pipeline instead of the Iran-Pakistan-India pipeline.'[329] Thus, it is clear that the development of Iran-India energy relations has faced many obstacles. However, except for limits placed on the Iran-India energy relations, the development of political relations with India in one of the goals on Iran's agenda.

5.2.
IRAN-INDIA POLITICAL RELATIONS

The main political goal of Iran's energy policy towards India is solving its international isolation and alleviate pressure from the Western states in relationship with the East and South Eastern Asian countries. Iran has tried to influence some countries, including India, so that they do not back the US policy towards Iran. Iran has applied its energy potential as the main tool in this context.

Iran tries to increase its oil exports to India and according to the Indian Ministry of External Affairs '...the years 2004–2005 saw further deepening and consolidation of India-Iran ties, with increased momentum of high-level exchanges and institutional linkages between their National Security Councils.'[330] However, it seems that the Iranian attempt was not enough to attain India's political support. India voted three times against Tehran in its nuclear dispute with the international community in 2005, 2006 and, 2009 at the International Atomic Energy Agency (IAEA), stood by the sanctions regime imposed by the UN Security Council, and openly proclaimed its opposition to the Iranian nuclear program.

---

[328] Sud 2008.

[329] Afrasiabi 2008.

[330] Kronstadt, Katzman 2006: 2.

The Iranian plan to develop political relations with India failed with the improving India–US relationship. The US-India 'global partnership' has been established through growing cooperation in areas of economics, energy, environment, democracy, non-proliferation and security, and high-technology and space. Meanwhile, the US, as India's new partner, has made Iran a test of credibility of New Delhi's commitment to build a long-term political partnership with Washington.[331]

Although India did not consider Iran to be an aggressive regional power, its relations with the US have affected New Delhi-Tehran relations and prevented further development of the India-Iran ties. In other words, the India-US relationship has tied India with US policies and, consequently, India has put better ties with Iran on hold.

However, some Indian leaders still argue that '…India's current relations with the United States will not weaken their own ties with Tehran.'[332] In addition, there is a constituency urging resistance to any US pressure that might inhibit the New Delhi-Tehran relations. But, '…India's IAEA votes demonstrate New Delhi's strategic choice to strengthen its partnership with Washington even at the cost of its friendship with Tehran.'[333]

The reasons behind India's policy towards Iran and its commitment to US can be analyzed based on India's new foreign policy under the new world order. The model of complex interdependence allows for the understanding of the opportunities and the constraints that come with India's new foreign policy.

5.3.
INDIA'S ECONOMIC REFORM AND ENERGY SECURITY

Like some other countries, India renewed its economic and foreign policy agendas, and entered an era of interdependence with economic liberalization in 1990. The liberalization process brought reforms in areas of foreign investment and capital markets, deregulating both the domestic business conditions and the country's trade regime.

The reforms raised India's attractiveness for investors, leading to a rise in foreign investment inflows. As a result, India has emerged as one of the perfect markets for foreign investors due to its vast market base. According to reports, the level of foreign direct investments rose from about $129 million in 1992 to about $2511 million in 1997.[334] In addition, data show that foreign

---

[331] Mohan 2008: 147.

[332] Indian Ministry of External Affairs *2004–2005*.

[333] Kronstadt, Katzman 2006: 3.

[334] Reserve Bank of India 2010.

investments in 1991 and 2000, in dollar terms, amounted to about $67 billion, at an average exchange rate of 40 rupees to a dollar.[335] The rate of (FDI) has grown by around 85.1% in 2009 to US $46.5 billion from US $25.1 billion.[336]

Moreover, liberalization has greatly improved the Indian economy and made it into a huge consumer market. India is the world's 12th largest economy in terms of market exchange rate and the 4th largest in terms of purchasing power parity.[337]

On the other hand, economic development has increased India's demand for energy. Its oil consumption grew from 1,190.00 bpd in 1991 to 2,147.00 bpd in 2000 and 2,702.00 in 2006.[338] India began to seek long-term arrangements to ensure its energy security. The Indian government launched some policies, such as a policy of energy import diversification and acquisition of equity in oil by India's state-owned oil companies. It also made efforts to build up a strategic petroleum reserve (SPR) in order to cope with sudden losses due to, for instance, a regional crisis in the Persian Gulf, to expand domestic exploration, and, lastly, to achieve a sufficient level of fuel production and fuel diversification.[339]

Although India has sought to attain energy security, the country's dependence on the international energy market has grown, making it more vulnerable. This is due to India's growing oil demand. '…India imported nearly 80% of its crude oil requirements in 2009, and the country spent almost $80 billion to import about 160 million tons of crude oil. Domestic oil production has stagnated at below 35 million tones.'[340]

Meanwhile, the Indian Prime Minster, Manmohan Sing warned that '…India's energy demands would increase by 40% over the next 10 years, whereas the increase in domestic production is likely to be a mere 12%, leading to a huge demand-supply mismatch'. Therefore, like China, another energy guzzling economy, India depends on oil imports from oil exporting countries in the Middle East as its possible long-term suppliers.[341] This policy led India to import oil from Iran and, as a result, Iran became India's second oil supplier in 2009.[342]

---

[335] Nagara 2003: 1703.

[336] Maps of India 2010.

[337] Rediff Business 2009.

[338] Index Mundi 2006.

[339] Wagner 2006: 4.

[340] Domain-b 2010.

[341] Kumaraswamy 2009: 4.

[342] Tehran Times 2010.

Although energy could be the source of progress in Iran-India relations, India has been concerned over the related political issues, which prevented it from expanding its relations with Iran. Its relationship with Iran is namely closely linked with Indian security and foreign policy issues.

## 5.4.
## INDIA-IRAN RELATIONS AND ECONOMIC INTERDEPENDENCE

Based on India's new policy in the post-Cold War world order, the country needs to cast its net in international relations as wide as possible in order to become a genuine regional and prospectively a global power. India has to develop its relations with the great powers because '…its new role in the international system is defined by its future economic, military, and technological capabilities that are regarded as the basis for great power status in the envisioned multi-polar system of the 21st century.'[343] Following this policy, India has created a series of strategic partnerships with the United States, France, Great Britain, Russia, China, the European Union, Germany and other countries.

India has probably benefited from the new complex interdependence relationships with the great powers. But these relationships have increased India's dependence on others, creating new constraints on its foreign policy. This is because India is a rising and ambitious power, while it is not in the same position compared with the great powers, such as Germany, France or even China in terms of various measures of 'hard power' military strength, economy, technology, and demographics. For instance '…India has yet to acquire the kind of economic clout that China already has. Furthermore, one of the criteria to be counted as major power surely ought to be the capacity to produce at home major weapons systems needed for modern warfare-fighter and bomber aircraft, long range artillery, tank and so on.'[344]

These factors have increased India's dependence on foreign suppliers and affected its foreign policy. As can be seen, India has been avoiding developing its multilateral and political relations with Iran. This is due to the fact that this could lead to a strain in its relations with the US, which is sticking to its policy of isolation towards Iran, also supported by the European countries. India is aware of the West's policy and, especially, the United States. They conduct their policy towards Iran through diplomatic and economic channels, international pressure and cross-societal exchanges. Thus, India would risk its interest in relations with the West, if it developed its relations with Iran.

---

[343] Wagner 2006: 8.

[344] Gharekhan 2009: xvii.

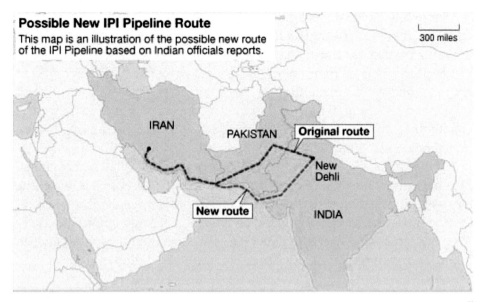

**Possible New IPI Pipeline Route**

This map is an illustration of the possible new route of the IPI Pipeline based on Indian officials reports.

300 miles

IRAN

PAKISTAN

Original route

New Dehli

New route

INDIA

*Map 3. Iran-Pakistan-India Gas Pipeline Project*
*Source: CIA*

India's vulnerability to complex interdependence can be seen in the Iran-Pakistan-India gas pipeline project. The pipeline issue implies further security and foreign policy considerations that might affect India's relations with the US and Europe. The pipeline project became closely intertwined with the international debate about Iran's nuclear program and relations with the US. Former US Secretary of State Condoleezza Rice declared in 2005 her country's opposition to the program because it would ostensibly strengthen Iran's power and thus negatively affect the United States politically.[345]

It needs to be kept in mind that the United States offered alternative energy sources to India if the country withdrew from the IPI project. As a matter of fact '...the civilian nuclear deal can, therefore, be seen in a larger context of Indo-US relations and the endeavors of the US to support India's energy needs whereas Iran touches relations with the United States.'[346]

Moreover, the US has tried to push India into forming relations with its partners in the Persian Gulf instead of relations with Iran. This, combined with the fact that the Arab states of the Persian Gulf would have to face most of the security consequences of a rising Iran, opens up new possibilities for Indian-US strategic cooperation in the Persian Gulf. Some US analysts recognize this as parallel interests of the US and Indian policies in the Persian Gulf.[347]

---

[345] Rajaee 2004.

[346] Wagner 2006: 7.

[347] Mohan 2008.

Meanwhile, political instability and even the threat of US or Israeli military retaliation against an Iranian provocation has made Iran a less than attractive partner for India. India's leaders have learned that they cannot rely on Iran as far as their energy needs are concerned. This is reflected in Indian energy supplies. India's petroleum imports from Iran account to less than 16%, with Saudi Arabia the largest supplier of hydrocarbons. Kuwait, Iraq, and the United Arab Emirates (UAE) are also among India's five largest trading partners.[348]

Some of India's leaders continue to believe, however, that '…despite all these difficulties, Iran still remains important to India because it is one of the very few countries, which is endowed with large quantities of oil and natural gas, and this is not something any Indian government could ignore, especially when the demand for energy is galloping.'[349] Cooperation prospects between the two nations have not really changed or improved though.

5.5.
CONCLUSION

Iran needs the huge Indian market and India wants to get the most benefits possible from Iran's rich energy resources. According to the Iranian perspective, an economic partnership with India, as a key regional player and emerging global economic power, can help the Islamic state win supporters in light of the 'policy of isolation' adopted against Iran by the United States and its European partners. Iran has, therefore, tried to improve its bilateral relations with India, both economically and politically.

India, due to its high energy needs, could benefit significantly from Iran's energy resources. But this would be risky from the perspective of its relationship with the US and Europe. In this light, India does not seem to be willing to pursue its relations with Iran at the cost of its cooperation with the West, especially given its growing economic interdependence. This economic dependence on the West makes its foreign policy vulnerable to the needs of these countries, especially the US.

In sum, Iran cannot develop deeper energy relations with India because of its conflict with the US and European countries, even though the Iran-India energy relationship could be justified given the simple demand-supply paradigm. It is, therefore, clear that, the 'Look to East' policy cannot fully serve Iran's national interests and remove its need of the West. It cannot by itself lead to a balanced foreign policy.

---

[348] Energy information Administration, China 2009.

[349] Kumaraswamy 2008: 4.

# Summary

This study clearly shows that Iran's energy policy towards China and India (1979–2010) can be viewed through the theory of complex interdependence. Accordingly, Iran's energy policy towards these two countries is affected by both international and internal factors. It is the interaction of these two groups of factors that defines more specifically the exact nature of Iran's policy in relation to each of the two Asian countries.

Iran's energy policy in relation with these two countries can be explained by theory of complex interdependence. This theory suggests that the Iranian energy policy is largely driven by international factors. This is to say, for instance, that powerful states are able to force weaker states into compliance. This also explains how the US used sanctions and pressure on its European partners that led to a reduction of trade with Iran. The US pressure was mainly focused in the Iranian energy sector, including investments in oil and gas fields. The US also enforced restrictions on the transfer of capital and technology between Iran and Europe. This issue has made the Iranians realize that they had no choice but to shift trade links away from the European continent towards Asia. East Asian countries, due to fast growth of their economies and rising demand for oil and gas, replaced Europe as Iran's key energy partners.

These developments explain why Iran has adopted its 'Look to East' policy, which generally prioritizes the strengthening and deepening of bilateral relations with the Asian countries. As a consequence, Iran has been attempting to make strategic regional alliances with countries, such as China and India, especially in the energy and transit sectors. It can be argued that the growth factor of the Asian nations, particularly China and India, and their resulting higher oil imports, can provide much of the needed respite to Iran not only to revive its global oil business but also to strengthen it. At a time when Iran faced increasing international isolation, its 'Look to East' policy served as a fine recipe for its stagnated oil business. The Asian nations offer promising and stable markets for Iran's future energy trade.

China, with its fast economic growth, has become Iran's second largest oil customer, playing an ever increasing role in Iran's energy policy. The Iran-China energy relations are based on the concept of interdependence, with one being the oil producer in need of foreign investment to rebuild and grow its industry and the other being a large oil consumer. In other words, China gives Iran the technology and investments needed to develop its oil sector. The growing link between the two has made China one of the largest customers of Iranian oil and Iran one of the largest oil exporters to China for many years to come. While energy is the key driver of the interdependence between the two, its dynamics seems to be spilling over to other areas, in which the two countries can cooperate, reaping further benefits from this strengthening relationship.

It should be noted that Iran had faced a severe crisis of its oil industry after the Revolution because of isolationist policy imposed by the US. The search for a good market for its oil has been Iran's most important objective since the country heavily relies on oil revenues. This means that its energy relations are based on economic interdependence. It needs to be kept in mind that interdependence is a good solution in that it can offer energy security to both the oil producer and the oil consumer.

Iran's energy relationship with India is a bit different, however. India needs oil and gas, but, in comparison with China, it is not in a position to participate in Iran's oil sector. At the same time, Iran needs the huge Indian market. And India, naturally, wants to benefit from Iran's energy resources.

Iran has also desired to an alliance with the East Asian countries, particularly China, to strengthen its position in relation to the US. It also wants India to weaken its support for the US. However, the US has been an important pillar of these two countries' foreign policies. Since the end of the Cold War, US-China relations have been defined by many issues, including economic interdependence. The areas of interest and conflict, however, will increasingly be linked to China's economic growth and determined through diplomatic and economic channels. Although the US has pressured China due to its energy relations with Iran, it has not been a source of conflict between the two countries. However, China has shown that it was not going to compromise its relationship with the United States by strengthening its ties with Iran.

Iran is, however, increasing its bilateral relations with India by leveraging its energy resources to create powerful economic incentives to increase state-to-state cooperation. India entered the process of interdependence with the launch of economic liberalization in 1991, which grew India's energy demand, making the country more economically dependent also on powers, such as the US. India does not, however, enjoy the type of global strategic salience (it is not a member of the Security Council that has the power of veto) that could allow it to protect and promote Iran's global rehabilitation. In consequence, this relationship cannot truly be viewed as interdependent.

This study makes it clear that China and the United States have already become significantly interdependent and India is on the same path as its economic dependence on the US continues to grow. This means that the observed interdependence between China and the US, as well India and the US, has prevented China and India from forming a strategic relationship with Iran with the US still focused on isolating Iran.

Iran's 'Look to East' policy cannot be, therefore, classified under the concept of economic interdependence in the new world order, which has shifted from the previously bipolar system to a system of growing economic interdependence ever since the end of the Cold War. Both China and India are part of this economically interdependent world system, making it impossible for Iran to meet its strategic aims by building bilateral relations with these two countries.

# Bibliography

BOOKS

Alnahas, I. 2007: Continuity and Change in the Revolutionary Iran Foreign Policy, PhD dissertation, Department of Political Science Morgantown, West Virginia

Amirahmadi, H. 1990: Revolution and Economic Transition: The Iranian Experience, State University of New York Press, New York

Arman, S. 1998: Macroeconomic Adjustments and Oil Revenue Fluctuations: The Case of Iran 1960–1990, a thesis submitted for a Doctor of Philosophy degree in the Department of Economics at the University of Newcastle upon Tyne

Beblawi, H., Luciani, G. 1987: The Rentier State. Nation, State and Integration in the Arab World, London

Bharier, J. 1971: Economic Development in Iran 1900–1970, Oxford University, London

Cordesman, A., Al-Rodhan, K. 2006: Iran's Weapons of Mass Destruction: The Real and Potential Threat, Center for Strategic & International Studies, Washington

Cordesman, A., Al-Rodhan, K. 2007: Iran's Military Forces and Warfighting Capabilities: The Threat in the Northern Gulf, Center for Strategic & International Studies, Washington

Energy Information Administration, China 2006: Country Analysis Briefs

Energy Information Administration, China 2007: Country Analysis Briefs

Energy Information Administration, China 2008: Country Analysis Briefs

Energy Information Administration, China 2009: Country Analysis Briefs

Energy Information Administration, Iran 2006: Country Analysis Briefs

Energy Information Administration, Iran 2007: Country Analysis Briefs

Energy Information Administration, Iran 2008: Country Analysis Briefs

Energy Information Administration, Iran 2009: Country Analysis Briefs

Garver, J. 2006: China and Iran: Ancient Partners in a Post-imperial World, University of Washington Press, Washington

Hasan, I. 2009: Believers and Brothers: A History of Uneasy Relationship, Author-House, Bloomington

Hershlag, Z.Y. 1964: Introduction to the Modern Economic History of the Middle East, E.J. Brill, Leiden

Huwaidin, M. 2002: China's Relations with Arabia and the Gulf, Routledge, Abingdon

Ibp Usa 2009: Doing Business and Investing in Iran Guide, International Business Publications, Washington

*Iran: Country Study Guide* 2003: Iran: Country Study Guide, International Business Publications, Washinghton DC

Issawi, C., Yeganeh, R. 1962: The Economics of Middle Eastern Oil, Praeger Publishers, New York

Keohane, K., Ney, J. 1977: Power and Interdependence: World Politics in Transition, Little Brown and Company, Boston

Keohane, R. 1986: Seven Theory of World Politics: Structural Realism and Beyond, New York Press, New York

Marketos, T.N. 2009: China's Energy Geopolitics: The Shanghai Cooperation Organization and Central Asia, *Routledge Contemporary China Series*, Routledge, London

Martin, V. 2013: Anglo-Iranian Relations since 1800, Routledge, London

Mohammadi, M. 2003: Iran's Foreign Policy: Doctrine and Issues, Dadgostar, Tehran

Waltz, K.N. 1979: Theory of International Politics, Addison-Wesley Press, Boston

Yates, D. 1996: The Rentier State in Africa: Oil Rent Dependency and Neo-Colonialism in the Republic of Gabon, Africa World Press, Trenton, NJ

Zoghi, I. 1997: The Political and Economic Issues of Iran's Oil, Pajang, Tehran

## ARTICLES AND CHAPTERS

Amirahmadi, H. 1995: The Political Economy of Iran's Oil Policy, [*in*:] Gillespie, K., Henry, C.M., Oil in New World Order, University Press of Florida, Florida, 185–226

Amirahmadi, H. 1996: Iran's development: evolution and challenges, *Third World Quarterly* 17/1, 123–147

Amuzegar, J. 2005: Iran's Oil Stabilization Fund: A Misnomer, *Middle East Economic Survey* XLVIII/47

Axworthy, M. 2008: Oil, Battleships and Revolution, *Spectator Business* 1, 50–51

Beblawi, H. 1990: The Rentier State in the Arab World, [*in*:] Luciani, G. (Ed.), The Arab State, Routledge, London, 85–98

Carey, J. 1974: Iran and Control of Its Oil Resources, *Political Science Quarterly* 89/1, 152–170

Dannreuther, R. 2003: Bridging the Gulf? Iran, Central Asia and the Persian Gulf, *The Review of International Affairs* 2/4, 32–46

Estelami, H. 1999: A Study of Iran's Responses to Economic Sanctions, *Middle East Review of International Affairs* 3/3, 51–61

Gharehbaghian, M. 1987: Oil Revenue and the Militarization of Iran 1960, *Social Scientist* 15/4/5, 87–100

Gharekhan, C. 2009: Foreword, [*in*:] Sikiri, R., Challenge and Strategy: Rethinking India's Foreign Policy, SAGE Publications, London, xvii

Gordon, P. 2007: America, Europe, and the Nuclear Challenge from Iran, paper presented at V Annual GMF U.S.-EU Think Tank Symposium, Washington DC, 17–18

Isiksal, H. 2004: To What Extend Complex Interdependence: Theorists Challenge to Structural Realist School of International Relations?, *Alternatives. Journal of International Relations* 3/2&3, 130–156

Islamic Republic News Agency 2004: Islamic Republic News Agency, 27 December 2004

Jaffe, A. 2002: Beijing's Oil Diplomacy, *Survival* 44/1, 115–133

Jin, L. 2005: Energy First: China and the Middle East, *Middle East Quarterly* 12/2, 3–10

Karl, T.L. 2007: Oil-Led Development: Social, Political, and Economic Consequences, [*in*:] Cleveland, C.J. (Ed.), Encyclopedia of Energy, Vol. 4, Elsevier Inc., Amsterdam-Boston, 2

Kissane, D. 2007: Realist Theory and Central & Eastern Europe after the Cold War, paper presented at the 3rd CEU Graduate Conference in the Social Sciences, Central European University, Budapest, 25–27

Leverett, F., Bader, J. 2005: Managing China-US Energy Competition in the Middle East, *The Washington Quarterly*, winter 2005, 187–201

Mahdavi, H. 1970: The Patterns and Problems of Economic Development in Rentier States: The Case of Iran, [*in*:] Cook, M.A. (Ed.), Studies in the Economic History of the Middle East, Oxford University Press, Oxford, 428–467

Majd, M. 1995: The 1951–53 Oil Nationalization Dispute and the Iranian Economy: A Rejoinder, *Middle Eastern Studies* 31/3, 449–459

Maleki, A. 2007: Energy Supply and Demand in Eurasia: Cooperation between EU and Iran, *China and Eurasia Forum Quarterly* 5/4, 103–113

*Iran lists 21 oil companies* 2007: Iran lists 21 oil companies for privatization, *Mehr News Agency*, 20 June 2007

Mohan, C. 2008: India's Quest for Continuity in the Face of Change, *Washington Quarterly*, autumn 2008, 143–153

Nagara, R. 2003: Foreign Direct Investment in India in the 1990s: Trends and Issues, *Economic and Political Weekly* 38/17, 1701–1712

Nye, J.S. 1976: Independence and Interdependence, *Foreign Policy* 22, 130–161

Pesaran, M. 1992: The Iranian Foreign Exchange Policy and the Black Market for Dollars, *Middle East Journal* 24/1, 101–125

Rajaee, B. 2004: The Political Evolution of the Islamic Republic and U.S. Foreign Policy after September 11, *Comparative Studies of South Asia, Africa and the Middle East* 24/1, 159–172

Rivlin, P. 2006: Iran's Energy Vulnerability, *The Middle East Review of International Affairs* 10/4, 103–116

Roshandel, J. 1996: Confidence Building Measures in the Persian Gulf, *Iranian Journal of International Affairs* 8/3, 627–642

Talmadge, C. 2008: Closing Times: Assessing the Iranian Threat to the Strait of Hormuz, *International Security* 33/1, 82–117

Vaezi, M. 2006: Participation in Energy, Cooperation Is Security: Interdependency of Iran and China, *Diplomatic Hamshahri Monthly*, 6 March 2006, 22–28

Ziegler, C. 2006: The Energy Factor in China's Foreign Policy, *Journal of Chinese Political Science* 11/1, 1–23


## INTERNET SOURCES

Afrasiabi, K. 2008: Iran holds key to India's energy insecurity, Asia Times, *http://www.atimes.com/atimes/Middle_East/JD30Ak02.html* (accessed October 11, 2010)

Alfoneh, A. 2010: How Intertwined Are the Revolutionary Guards in Iran's Economy?, American Enterprise Institute for Public Policy Research, *http://www.aei.org/outlook/26991* (accessed September 10, 2010)

Amirahmadi, H. 2010: Iran's Power Structure, *http://www.iranian.com/Mar96/Opinion/AmirIran.html* (accessed May 10, 2010)

Ashagh, Y. 2010: Mehr News Agency, *http://www.mehrnews.com/fa/newsdetail.aspx?NewsID=1232542* (accessed December 10, 2011)

Badakhshan, M., Najmabadi, F. 2004: Encyclopedia Iranica, *http://www.iranicaonline.org/articles/oil-industry-i* (accessed November 14, 2010)

Bakhtiar, A. 2007: Ahmadinejad's Achilles Heel: The Iranian Economy, Payvand, 25 January 2007, *http://www.payvand.com/news/07/jan/1295.html* (accessed November 10, 2010)

Barzegar, K. 2008: Iran Eyes the China Card, Op-Ed, Post Global, A Conversation on Global Issues with David Ignatius and Fareed Zakaria, *http://belfercenter.ksg.harvard.edu/publication/18033/iran_eyes_the_china_card.html* (accessed July 2, 2009)

Bayegan, R. 2008: Iran's New Oil Disorder – An Interview with Dr Parviz Mina, Ekbatan Observer, *http://bayegan.blogspot.com/2005/08/irans-new-oil-disorder-interview-with.html* (accessed November 4, 2008)

Blank, S. 2006: China's Emerging Energy Nexus with Central Asia, *China Brief* 6/15, *http://www.jamestown.org/programs/chinabrief/single/?tx_ttnews%5Btt_news%5D=31886&tx_ttnews%5BbackPid%5D=196&no_cache=1* (accessed February 10, 2007)

Blumenthal, D. 2010: China's Grand Strategy, Foreign Policy, *http://shadow.foreignpolicy.com/posts/2010/04/29/china_s_grand_strategy* (accessed April 29, 2010)

*Bonyad-e Mostazafan*: Bonyad-e Mostazafan Islamic Republic of Iran, *www.irmf.ir/english/NewsFullStory.aspx?nid=1* (accessed January 5, 2010)

Brenner, L. 2001: The U.S.-P.R.C. Relationship from Realism to Complex Interdependence, Department of Politics and Public Administration University of Hong Kong, *http://www.leejbrenner.com/U.S.-P.R.C._Relations.html* (accessed September 9, 2007)

Brumberg, D., Ahram, A. 2007: Market and Politics, Georgetown University Prepared for the Baker Institute Energy Forum Rice University Houston, *www.rice.edu/energy/publications/docs/NOCs/Presentations/Hou-Brumberg-Iran.pdf* (accessed October 16, 2010)

Calabrese, J. 2006: China and Iran: Mismatched Partners, *www.1913intel.com/2006/08/18/china-and-iran-mismatched-partners* (accessed May 5, 2006)

Ceragioli, P., Martellini, M. 2003: The geopolitics of pipelines, Asia Times, 29 May 2003, *http://www.atimes.com/ atimes/Middle_East/EE29Ak05.html* (accessed February 15, 2008)

Chang, P. 2008: China's Policy toward Iran: Arms for Oil?, *China Brief* 8/21, *http://www.jamestown.org/programs/chinabrief/single/?tx_ttnews%5Btt_news%5D=34141&tx_ttnews%5BbackPid%5D=168&no_cache=1* (accessed June 10, 2008)

Chang, P. 2009: China's Policy toward Iran and the Middle East, Global Briefing, *http://www.jinsa.org/node/1221* (accessed November 24, 2009)

CIA World Factbook 1987: Iran's Oil Export, The Library of Congress Country Studies, *https://www.cia.gov/library/publications/the-world-factbook/docs/history.html* (accessed May 11, 2011)

CIA World Factbook 2008: U.S. Dept. of State Country Background Notes, *http://globaledge.msu.edu* (accessed June 12, 2010)

Clawson, P. 2010: U.S. Sanctions, Iranprimer, *http://iranprimer.usip.org/resource/us-sanctions* (accessed May 10, 2010)

*Constitution of Iran*: Constitution of Iran, *http://www.wipo.int/edocs/lexdocs/laws/en/ir/ir001en.pdf* (accessed Septmber 10, 2010)

Cordesman, A. 2007: Iran, Oil, and the Strait of Hormuz, Center for Strategic and International Studies, Arleigh A. Burke Chair in Strategy, *http://csis.org/files/media/csis/pubs/070326_iranoil_hormuz.pdf* (accessed June 15, 2008)

Daniel, B. 2010: China's Grand Strategy, *Foreign Policy*, *http://shadow.foreignpolicy.com/posts/2010/04/29/china_s_grand_strategy* (accessed May 29, 2010)

Daojiong, Z. 2008: Energy Interdependence, *China Security*, summer 2006, *http://www.issuelab.org/resources/371/371.pdf* (accessed May 10, 2011)

Domain-b 2010: PM warns of hydrocarbons demand-supply mismatch, 1 November 2010, *http://www.domain-b.com/industry/oil_gas/20101101_manmohan_singh.html* (accessed July 9, 2010)

Dorraj, M., Currier, C. 2008: Lubricated with Oil: Iran-China Relations in a Changing World, Middle East Policy Council, *http://www.mepc.org/journal/middle-east-policy-archives/lubricated-oil-iran-chinarelations-changing-world* (accessed August 10, 2010)

Dubowitz, M. 2010: The Sanctions on Iran are Working, *Foreign Policy*, *http://www.foreignpolicy.com/articles/2010/02/10/the_sanctions_on_iran_are_working?page=0,0* (accessed September 13, 2010)

Dumbaugh, K. 2005: China-US Relations: Current Issues and Implications for US Policy, CRS Report for Congress, Received through the CRS Web, *http://www.policyarchive.org/handle/10207/bitstreams/2363.pdf* (accessed April 3, 2005)

Economic Cooperation Organization 2009–2010: Trade and Development Bank, Iran Country Partnership Strategy, 3–9, *http://www.etdb.org/StrategiesAndResearch/Countries/CSPReports/ReportsLibrary/IRAN.pdf* (accessed May 14, 2010)

EIA International Petroleum Monthly: EIA International Petroleum Monthly, *http://www.eia.gov/petroleum/supply/monthly/* (accessed April 15, 2010)

*Encyclopaedia Iranica*: Encyclopaedia Iranica, *http://www.iranicaonline.org/articles/economy-ix* (accessed July 10, 2013)

Eshagh, Y.A.: Mehr News Agency, *http://www.mehrnews.com/fa/newsdetail.aspx?NewsID=1232542* (accessed May 12, 2011)

European Commission 2003: Trade Issues, Iran, *http://ec.europa.eu* (accessed May 10, 2010)

Fair, C. 2007: Indo-Iranian Ties: Thicker Than Oil, *Middle East Review of International Affairs*, *http://meria.idc.ac.il/journal/2007/issue1/jv11no1a9.html* (accessed July 7, 2007)

Fayazmanesh, S. 2002: The Politics of the U.S. Economic Sanctions against Iran, Department of Economics, California State University, *http://zimmer.csufresno.edu/~sasanf/MES101Documents/ThePoliticsOfUSEconSanctionsEconLit.pdf* (accessed January 10, 2010)

Federation of American Scientists 2008: Shahab-3 / Zelzal-3', *http://www.fas.org/programs/ssp/man/militarysumfolder/shahab-3.html* (accessed September 10, 2010)

Feiler, G. 2010: Iran and the West: Who Needs Whom? A Look at the Consequences of Ahmadinejad's Economic and Foreign Policies, BESA Perspectives, *http://www.biu.ac.il/SOC/besa/perspectives14.html* (accessed September 3, 2010)

Franssen, H., Morton, E. 2002: A Review of US Unilateral Sanctions against Iran, *Middle East Economic Survey*, *http://www.mafhoum.com/press3/108E16.htm* (accessed March 20, 2010)

Ghaninejad, M. 2008: An Interview with Dr. Mousa Ghaninejad, an interview by Eslam Mina, *www.irdiplomacy.ir/index.php?Lang=en&Page=21&TypeId=13&ArticleId=2902&Action=ArticleBodyView - 44k* (accessed May 12, 2008)

Ghezelbash, A. 2005: The Oil Weapon, *Heartland Magazine*, Unveiling Iran, 20–29, *http://www.tritaparsi.com/2005_04_unveiling_iran.pdf* (accessed November 12, 2010)

Ghorban, N. 2005: The Need to Restructure Iran's Petroleum Industry (Revisited after Eight Years), *Middle East Economic Survey* XLVIII/24, *http://www.gasandoil.com/news/2005/07/ntm52712* (accessed May 7, 2011)

Guillaume, D., Zytek, R. 2011: The Economics of Energy Price Reform in the Islamic Republic of Iran, International Monetary Fund, 2, *http://imf.org/external/
pubs/ft/scr/2010/cr1076.pdf* (accessed February 11, 2011)

Hafezi, M., Mostashari, A., Alvandi, R. 2004: The Impact of U.S. Sanctions on Iran:
Economic and Social Assessmen, Iranian Studies Group at MIT, *www.isgmit.
org* (accessed March 11, 2010)

*High Oil Price*: High Oil Price Undermines Economy, an interview with Kamal
Daneshyar, *Iran International Magazine, http://www.iraninternationalmagazine.
com/issue_39/text/high%20oil%20price.htm* (accessed June 11, 2009)

*History of Iran*: History of Iran, Iran Chamber, *http://www.iranchamber.com/history/
oil_nationalization/oil_nationalization.php* (accessed June 18, 2010)

Hooshiyar, K. 2010: Iran, globalization, and US imperialist agenda in the Middle East,
*Iran Review, www.iranreview.com/Editorials/Iran%20and%20US.pdf* (accessed May
20, 2011)

Indian Ministry of External Affairs 2004–2005: Annual Report 2004–2005, *http://www.
mea.gov.in/meaxpsite/annualreport/30ar01.pdf* (accessed February 10, 2010)

*International Energy Outlook* 2009: International Energy Outlook 2009, *http://www.world-
energyoutlook.org/media/weowebsite/2009/WEO2009.pdf* (accessed July 11, 2010)

*International Energy Outlook* 2010: International Energy Outlook 2010, *http://www.
reliabilityweb.com/index.php/articles/us_energy_information_administration_in-
ternational_energy_outlook_2010/* (accessed July 10, 2010)

Index Mundi 2006: India Crude Oil Consumption by Year, *http://www.indexmundi.com/en-
ergy.aspx?country=in&product=oil&graph=consumption* (accessed September 11, 2010)

Jahanbegloo, R. 2005: Who is in Charge in Iran, Heartland Magazine, Unveiling
Iran, 6–13 www.tritaparsi.com (accessed September 10, 2010)

Junbo, J. 2010: Iran vote shows China's Western drifts, Asia Times, *http://www.
atimes.com/atimes/China/LF25Ad02.html* (accessed June 25, 2010)

Katzman, K. 2007: The Iran Sanctions Act (ISA), CRS Report for Congress, *http://
www.coherentbabble.com/CRS/CRS-RS20871-12507.pdf* (accessed May 15, 2010)

Kazemi, A. 2010: Political Constraints of Iran's Economic Reform, Middle East
Academic Forum, 27 December 2010, *https://www.academia.edu/7093462/Po-
litical_Constraints_of_Iran_s_Economic_Reform* (accessed July 11, 2011)

Kemenade, W. 2009: Iran's Relations with China and the West Cooperation and
Confrontation in Asia, Netherlands Institute of International Relations Clin-
gendael, *www.clingendael.nl/publications/2009/20091100cdsp_paper_kemenade_
iran.pdf* (accessed October 6, 2010)

Khalaji, M.: Iranian President Ahmadinezhad's Relations with Supreme Leader
Khamenei, The Washington Institute for Near East Policy, *http://www.wash-
ingtoninstitute.org/policy-analysis/view/iranian-president-ahmadinezhads-rela-
tions-with-supreme-leader-khamenei* (accessed September 10, 2009)

Kiernan, P. 2007: Iran, Sanctions and War: The Oil Factor, World Politics Review Exclusive, *http://www.worldpoliticsreview.com/article.aspx?id=1247* (accessed July 17, 2007)

Kronstadt, A., Katzman, K. 2006: India-Iran Relations and U.S. Interests, Congressional Research Service, *http://www.usembassy.it/pdf/other/RS22486.pdf* (accessed October 8, 2010)

Kumaraswamy, P. 2009: India's Persian Problems, Strategic Insights, *http://www.ccc.nps.navy.mil/si/2008/Jul/kumaraswamyJul08.asp* (accessed May 10, 2010)

Leverett, F., Leverett, H. 2009: Understanding China's Iran Policy, Race for Iran, *http://www.raceforiran.com/understanding- chinas-iran-policy* (accessed September 16, 2009)

Ma, X. 2008: China's Energy Strategy in The Middle East, *Middle East Economic Survey* LI/ 23, *https://www.thefreelibrary.com/China's+energy+security%3A+challenges+and+opportunities.-a0235406711* (accessed September 10, 2010)

Maleki, A. 2007: Iran's New Asian Identity,[in:] Novikova,G., Regional Security Issues, Yerevan, Amrost Group. *www.caspianstudies.com* (accessed May 11, 2015)

Maleki, A. 2010: Iran's nuclear file: recommendations for the future, American Academy, *http://www.amacad.org/content/publications/pubContent.aspx?d=885* (accessed June 10, 2011)

Maleki, A. 2010: Iran's Regional Foreign Energy Policy, Caspian Studies, *www.caspianstudies.com* (accessed May 11, 2015)

Maps of India 2010: Globalization and Liberalization, *http://business.mapsofindia.com/globalization/liberalization.html* (accessed September 21, 2008)

McCartan, B. 2008: Myanmar Signs up Energy Partners, Asia Times *http://www.atimes.com/atimes/Southeast_Asia/JG10Ae01.html* (accessed May 10, 2010)

McLaughlin, K. 2006: Centuries-old partnership binds China, Iran together, *http://www.sfgate.com/cgi-bin/article.cgi?file=/c/a/2006/09/18/MNGJPL7MQ41.DTL* (accessed September 18, 2006)

Metz, H. (Ed.) 1987: Iran: A Country Study, Washington: GPO for the Library of Congress, *http://countrystudies.us/iran/* (accessed July 5, 2010)

Ministry of Commerce 2009: The Foreign Trade Regime of the Islamic Republic of Iran, *www.irantradelaw.com/wp-content/uploads/2010/03/Irans-Foreign-Trade-Regime-Report.pdf* (accessed May 10, 2011)

Ministry of Foreign Affairs 2010: The People's Republic of China, *http://www.fmprc.gov.cn/eng/ziliao/3602/3604/t18001.htm* (accessed January 15, 2010)

Mohaddesa, K., Pesaran, M. 2014: One Hundred Years of Oil Income and the Iranian Economy: A Curse or a Blessing?, *http://www.econ.cam.ac.uk/people/cto/km418/100_Iranian_Oil.pdf* (accessed October 10, 2014)

Nader, A. 2011: Iran Overhauls Subsidies in the Face of Sanctions, *http://www.rand.org/commentary/2011/01/13/GS.html* (accessed September 09, 2011)

Nikou, S. 2011: Iran's Subsidies Conundrum, United States Institute of Peace, *http://www.usip.org/files/resources/pb49_0.pdf* (accessed July 9, 2011)

Nili, M. 2010: Picture of Iran's Oil-Dependent Economy, Iranian International Magazine, *http://www.iraninternationalmagazine.com/issue_40/text/picture%20 of%20 iran's%20oil.htm* (accessed August 20, 2010)

NIOC 2007: National Iranian Oil Company, *http://www.nioc.ir* (accessed December 7, 2007)

NIOC 2008: National Iranian Oil Company, 1 June 2008, *http://www.nioc.ir* (accessed May 7, 2009)

*Oil & Gas in Iran* 2012: Oil & Gas in Iran, Petropars, retrieved 19 January 2012, *http://www.nioc.ir* (accessed July 11, 2013)

Ong, L. 2004: China, India: Difference in the Details, Asia Times, *http://www. atimes.com/atimes/China/FD30Ad04.html* (accessed April 11, 2010)

OPEC 2004: Annual Statistical Bulletin, *http://www.opec.org/opec_web/en/publica-tions/202.htm* (accessed March 9, 2010)

OPEC 2016: Annual Statistical Bulletin, *http://www.opec.org/opec_web/en/about_ us/163.htm* (accessed September 15, 2016)

Payvand's Iran News 2008: Iran Plans to Boost Crude Exports to China, India, *http://www.payvand.com/news/08/aug/1265.html* (accessed May 25, 2008)

Press TV 2007: Italy, Iran's main EU trade partner, 19 June 2007, *http://www.presstv. ir/detail.aspx?id=13680&sectionid=351020102* (accessed October 25, 2008)

Press TV 2008: Iran has OPEC's 3rd top oil income, 28 July 2008, *http://edition. presstv.ir/detail/64997.html* (accessed June 25, 2010)

Rediff Business 2009: The world's largest economies, *http://business.rediff.com/ slide-show/2009/nov/27/slide-show-1-the-worlds-largest-economies.htm* (accessed February 12, 2010)

Reference for Business: National Iranian Oil Company, *www.referenceforbusiness.com/ history2/75/NATIONAL-IRANIAN-OIL-COMPANY.html* (accessed July 10, 2011)

Reserve Bank of India 2010: Foreign investment in India, *http://www.indiaonestop. com/economy-fdi.htm* (accessed February 10, 2010)

Reuters 2009: FACTBOX: Iran's Major Oil Customers, Energy Partners, 28 August 2009, *http://www.reuters.com/article/idUSTRE57H1UJ20090818* (accessed June 11, 2010)

Richardson, M. 2008: Middle East Balancing Act is Becoming Harder for China, The Canberra Times, *http://www.canberratimes.com.au/news/opinion/editorial/general/ middle-east- balancing-act-is-becoming-harder-for-china/1228193.aspx* (accessed July 28, 2008)

Saghafi, N. 2008: Iran and look to the East policy, Centre for Strategic Research, *http://www.csr.ir/PDF/Issues102/PeriodicalIssues_1.pdf* (accessed April 5, 2010)

Sahimi, M. 2003: Iran's Nuclear Program, Payvand's Iran News, *http://www.pay-vand.com/news/05/sep/1070.html* (accessed May 16, 2010)

Sajadiyan, V. 2009: Hydrocarbon Reservoirs, [*in:*] Report of Specialized Session on 'Strategic Issues Related to Energy Sector', *http://www.csr.ir/center.aspx?lng=en&subid=-1&&cntid=1569* (accessed June 20, 2009)

Sariolghalam, M. 2007: Let's See the World as an Opportunity, Not a Threat, Iran Diplomacy, 9 June 2007, *http://irdiplomacy.com/en/page/1106/Let%E2%80%99s+See+the+World+as+an+Opportunity%2C+Not+a+Threat.html* (accessed June 20, 2011)

Sokolski, H. 2000: Prevailing in a Well-Armed World: Devising Competitive Strategies against Competitive Strategies, Strategic Studies Institute, *http://www.strategicstudiesinstitute.army.mil/pdffiles/00293.pdf* (accessed March 20, 2010)

Sud, H. 2008: India looks to Central Asia for energy, United Press International, *http://www.upiasia.com/Economics/2008/06/17/india_looks_to_central_asia_for_energy/5733/* (accessed July 17, 2010)

Tehran Times 2010: Iran Sanctions Could Hit Major Oil Firms, 3 March 2010, *http://www.tehrantimes.com/index_View.asp?code=215230* (accessed February 10, 2010)

Thompson, E.V: A Brief History of Major Oil Companies in the Gulf Region, Petroleum Archives Project, Arabian Peninsula & Gulf Studies Program, University of Virginia, *http://www.virginia.edu/igpr/APAG/apagoilhistory.html* (accessed September 5, 2012)

Toichi, T. 2008: Asian Energy Demand and Competition, lecture delivered on 2–4 June 2008 at Asia's Strategic Challenges, International Institute for Strategic Studies, Tokyo, *http://eneken.ieej.or.jp/en/data/pdf/441.pdf* (accessed May 10, 2011)

Tung, C. 2002: The Impact of Bilateral Economic Interdependence on US-China Relations, *http://citation.allacademic.com/meta/p_mla_apa_research_citation/0/7/0/5/0/pages70506/p70506-1.php* (accessed December 15, 2010)

Vaezi, M.: Iran's Constructive Foreign Policy under the 20-Year Vision Plan, Center for Strategic Research, *http://www.csr.ir/departments.aspx?lng=en&abtid=06&&depid=74&semid=1679* (accessed July 10, 2010)

Vaezi, M. 2006: An Asian Dialogue on Energy Security: A Model for Interdependence, Center for Strategic Research, *http://www.csr.ir/departments.aspx?lng=en&abtid=07&depid=74&semid=531* (accessed September 8, 2006)

Wagner, C. 2006: Welcome to Interdependence, Energy, Security and Foreign Policy, German Institute for International and Security Affairs, *https://www.swp-berlin.org/fileadmin/contents/products/arbeitspapiere/2006_2Wgn_ks.pdf* (accessed June 10, 2009)

Wakefield, B., Hathaway, R. 2010: China and the Persian Gulf, *http://www.dw-world.de/dw/article/05793782,00.html* (accessed April 12, 2010)

Wellman, A., Frasco, R. 2011: China-Iran Foreign Relations, *http://www.irantracker.org/foreign-relations/china-iran-foreign-relations* (accessed September 10, 2011)

The World Bank: The World Bank, *http://data.worldbank.org/indicator/NY.GDP.DEFL.KD.ZG* (accessed August 10, 2013)

World Economic Report 1950–1951: Summary of Recent Economic Development in the Middle East, 49–50, *http://www.un.org/en/development/desa/policy/wess/wess_archive/1950_1951wes_middleeast_summary.pdf* (accessed July 1, 2014)

Word Press 2015: Word Press, *https://arirusila.wordpress.com/category/energy-policy/* (accessed December 3, 2015)

Worth, R. 2010: Ayatollah Supports Bid to Sharply Cut Iran Subsidies, New York Times, *http://www.nytimes.com/2010/04/06/world/middleeast/06iran.html?_r=1* (accessed May 4, 2010)

Xia, Y. 2008: The Cold War and Chinese Foreign Policy, IR International Relations, *http://www.e-ir.info/?p=518* (accessed May 16, 2008)

Yan, Z. 2008: Chin's Energy Needs and Central Asia, National Observer, *http://goliath.ecnext.com/coms2/gi_0199-5472099/China-s-energy-needs-and.html* (accessed August 22, 2006)

Young, W. 2010: Gas Prices Soar in Iran as Subsidy Is Reduced, New York Times, *http://www.nytimes.com/2010/12/20/world/middleeast/20iran.html?_r=1* (accessed May 12, 2010)

Your Petrochemical News 2008: Twenty petrochemical companies to be privatized in Iran, 25 September 2008, *http://www.yourpetrochemicalnews.com/news_item.php?newsID=11321* (accessed February 8, 2009)

# Anex 1
# List of Iran's energy partners in 2007

The following details Iran's principal energy partners and joint projects published by Alexander's Gas & Oil Connections at www.gasandoil.com

## Asia
### Japan
- Biggest single buyer of Iran's crude. Imported over 400,000 bpd in the second quarter 2008. Iran was Japan's fourth-largest supplier. Nippon oil is the largest importer of Iran's oil, taking 100,000 to 120,000 bpd.

Investment
- Japan's Inpex Holdings saw its 75% stake in Iran's huge Azadegan oilfield cut to 10% in 2006 when talks fell through on a development plan.

### China
- Second-largest buyer of Iran's oil. Imported just under 400,000 bpd in the second quarter 2008. Iran is China's third largest crude supplier. China's state-run Zhuhai Zhenrong lifts around 240,000 bpd, while China's top refiner Sinopec Corp buys around 160,000 bpd. Zhenrong delivers its crude to Sinopec, the only Chinese refiner that processes Iranian oil.

Investment
- Sinopec finalized a $2 billion pact to develop Iran's huge Yadavaran field in December.
- The China National Offshore Oil Corp (CNOOC) is in talks to finalize a $16 billion deal to develop the North Pars gas field and build a liquefied natural gas (LNG) plant.
- CNPC is in talks with Iran on a $3.6 billion deal to buy LNG from Phase 14 of the South Pars project. CNPC is also in talks to explore and develop energy reserves in Iran's Caspian.

### India
- Imports around 360,000 bpd of Iranian crude. The biggest importer is refiner MRPL with around 130,000 bpd. Reliance imports around 120,000 bpd of Iran's oil and is expected to buy more for its new 580,000 bpd refinery in Jamnagar. India supplies much of Iran's imported oil gasoline and diesel.

Investment

- India's ONGC, IOC and Oil India Ltd are in talks to invest $3 billion to develop gas reserves at the Farsi block.
- ONGC and the Hinduja group are negotiating for a role in Azadegan oilfield development and to buy gas from South Pars. ONGC is in talks to develop Caspian oil and gas reserves.
- India is negotiating for gas through a proposed pipeline via Pakistan.
- India's Essar plans to help build a 300,000 bpd refinery in Bandar Abbas worth up to $10 billion.

## Malaysia

- SKS signed a multi-billion-dollar development deal in December 2007 to develop Golshan and Ferdows gas fields. Initial investment would be at $6 billion. SKS also plans an LNG plant.
- SKS and Iran's state oil firm NIOC plan to build a 200,000 bpd oil refinery in Malaysia to process Iranian crude.
- National oil firm Petronas has a 10% stake in Pars LNG project and is assessing its role after Total halted spending on Iran gas.

## Indonesia

- State oil firm Pertamina and Iran plan to build a 300,000 bpd refinery in Indonesia. Indonesia is also involved in the construction of 360,000 bpd gas condensate splitter at Bandar Abbas in Iran.

## Pakistan

- Negotiating for gas supplies through proposed pipeline to India.

South Korea

- Imported up to 232,000 bpd of Iran's oil in 2007. Hyundai Oilbank and SK Energy both imported around 116,000 bpd.

## Taiwan

- Imported 86,000 bpd of Iran's oil in the second quarter.

## Russia

- Russia is building Iran's first nuclear power plant and supplying the fuel for its use.
- Russia's state-controlled energy giant Gazprom agreed in February to take on new projects in Iran, including a bigger role in South Pars and drilling for oil. Gazprom has invested about $4 billion in Iran since 2007 and was involved in an earlier phase at South Pars.

## Europe

- Austria's biggest energy company OMV is leading a consortium that plans to build the Nabucco pipeline to carry gas from central Asia to Europe by 2013. Europe wants the pipeline to diversify supplies and ease dependence on Russia but without Iran, it will be difficult to fill the $8 billion pipeline.

  OMV signed a preliminary deal last year to develop part of South Pars and build an LNG terminal. The US has criticized the deal. OMV is also developing Iran's Mehr oilfield with Spain's Repsol and Chile's Sipetrol.

## France

- French oil giant Total buys around 80,000 bpd of Iran's crude for its refining system.

Investment

- Total put new investments in Iran on hold in July due to international political tension. It had a preliminary agreement to develop phase 11 of South Pars and to build an LNG plant to export the gas. Total has previously invested at least $4 billion in Iran.

## Italy

- Refiners ERG, ENI and API import a combined total of over 80,000 bpd of Iranian crude.

Investment

- ENI is leading the $1 billion second phase development of the Darkhovin oil field to take output to 160,000 bpd from 50,000 bpd. Iran has asked ENI to plan a third phase to lift output by another 100,000 bpd. ENI has invested at least $5 billion in energy projects in Iran, according to industry estimates.

## Poland

- Polish gas monopoly PGNiG signed a preliminary agreement in February with the Iranian Offshore Oil Company to help manage reserves of natural gas and condensates.

## Spain

- Spanish refiners Repsol and Cepsa import a combined total of over 100,000 bpd of Iranian crude.

Investment

- Repsol had planned to participate with Shell in developing South Pars and building an LNG plant, but Shell pulled out in May.

### Switzerland

- Swiss utility EGL signed a 25-year gas purchase deal worth over $13 billion with Iran in March. EGL said it could get the first gas through the deal via pipelines next year.

### Turkey

- Turkish refiner Tupras imports around 130,000 bpd of Iranian crude.

Investment

- Turkey signed a preliminary deal last year for gas to be exported to Europe through Turkey and for Turkey to produce gas in the South Pars field. The investment would amount to $3.5 billion.

### UK

- Royal Dutch Shell buys about 100,000 bpd of Iran's crude for its refining system. BP buys about 25,000 bpd.

Investment

- Shell pulled out of a plan to develop a phase at South Pars and build an LNG terminal. Shell has said it may yet get involved in a later phase.

# Aneks 2
# List of companies that invested in Iran's energy sector (1996–2007)
published by HONESTLY CONCERNED E.V.

*http://honestlyconcerned.info/2007/03/23/some-companies-investing-in-irans-energy-sector/*

## Total (France)
- In September 1997, Total signed a $2 billion contract along with Gazprom and Petronas Malaysia to develop phases 2 and 3 of the South Pars natural gas field. Total has since expanded its involvement to other portions of the South Pars fields (Congressional Research Service, August 2006).
- In February 1999 Total and ENI began operating in Iran's Doroud oil field with an investment of $1 billion. Total is operator of the project, with a 55% share, while ENI holds the other 45% (Energy Information Agency, Department of Energy, August 2006).
- In April 1999, Iran awarded Total a 46.75% stake to develop the off-shore Balal field. Bow Valley Energy and ENI are also invested in the field, a reported total of $300 million (Energy Information Agency, Department of Energy, August 2006).
- Note: In 2000 Elf Aquitaine merged with Total Fina to form TotalFinaElf, which changed its name to Total in 2003. The investments made prior to 2000 were done separately by the two companies but are now under the control of the merged corporation.

## Royal Dutch Shell (Dutch)
- In November 1999, Shell signed an agreement with the National Iranian Oil Company (NIOC) to develop two offshore oil fields in the Persian Gulf, Soroush and Nowruz. Shell's investment of more than $800 million was pivotal in raising Iran's oil output by 190,000 barrels per day – p about an 8% increase in total Iranian output. In mid-2005 Shell handed over the two developed fields to Iran after development difficulties forced the company to halt production. Shell, however, remained involved in the marketing of the oil from the fields (Congressional Research Service, August 2006).

- Shell is also involved in negotiations with the Iranian government and China's Sinopec regarding a 20% equity stake in the Yadavaran oil field in southern Iran (International Oil Daily, November 7, 2006).
- In January 2007, Shell, in partnership with Repsol, signed a preliminary deal to develop sections 13 and 14 of the South Pars field. The project would involve building a plant capable of liquefying 8- million tons of natural gas a year for shipment to Europe and elsewhere. According to the Iranians, the deal is valued at $10 billion (The Associated Press, January 30, 2007).
- In January 2001 Enterprise Oil took a 20% stake in phases 6, 7, and 8 of the South Pars natural gas field. After Shell purchased Enterprise it withdrew from the development.

### Repsol (Spain)
- In October 2004, Repsol signed a $27 million deal with the National Iranian Oil Company (NIOC) for exploration operations in Forouz and Iran-Mehr oil blocs in southern Iran (Iranian Student News Agency, October 15, 2004).
- In October 2001, Repsol in conjunction with OMV, ENAP (through its subsidiary Sipetrol) signed an agreement to explore the Mehr oil block. In February 2007 the block was declared commercial with recoverable reserves of 150 million barrels (Platts Oilgram News, February 2, 2007).
- In January 2007, Repsol, in partnership with Shell, signed a preliminary deal to develop sections 13 and 14 of the South Pars field. The project would involve building a plant capable of liquefying 8 million tons of natural gas a year for shipment to Europe and elsewhere. According to the Iranians, the deal is valued at $10 billion (The Associated Press, January 30, 2007).

### ENI (Italy)
- In February 1999 ENI, in conjunction with Total, began operating in Iran's Doroud oil field with an investment of $1 billion (Energy Information Agency, Department of Energy, August 2006).
- In April 1999, Iran awarded ENI a 38.25% stake to develop the offshore Balal field. In April 1999, Iran awarded Bow Valley a 15% stake to develop the offshore Balal field. Total and ENI are also invested in the field a reported total of $300 million (Energy Information Agency, Department of Energy, August 2006).
- In July 2000, ENI invested in Phase 4 and 5 of the South Pars natural gas project in a deal estimated to be worth $1.9 billion (Energy Information Agency, Department of Energy, August 2006).

- In June 2001 ENI signed a $1 billion contract to explore Iran's Dark-hovin oil field (Energy Information Agency, Department of Energy, August 2006).

## INPEX (Japan)

- In January 2003, JAPEX and INPEX participated in the development project of the Soroosh and Nowrooz fields through joint investment in JJI S&N, which holds a 20% working interest in the project (INPEX Website, retrieved March 19, 2007).
- In 2004 INPEX signed an agreement to develop the Azadegan oil field. Under the agreement INPEX held a 75% stake in the $2 billion project and the other 25% share was held by the National Iranian Oil Company (NIOC). In October 2006 fears that the deal may lead to US sanctions caused the deal to be slashed with INPEX now holding only a 10% stake (Congressional Research Service, August 2006 & International Oil Daily, October 10, 2006).

## Oil and Natural Gas Company, ONGC, Indian Oil Corporation (IOC) and Oil India Ltd (India)

- ONGC is involved in the exploration of the Farsi Block. In 2002, a consortium of Indian companies signed a contract to carry out exploration in the Farsi Block. The consortium consists of ONGC-Videsh with 40%, IOC with 40% and OIL with 20% of the equity. The contract commits $27 million in exploration obligation. Oil discovery in excess of 500 million barrels is expected. In November 2006, it was reported the consortium struck oil at three offshore exploration wells in the Farsi block (UPI, November 15, 2006 & The Telegraph [Calcutta] December 27, 2002).
- In October 2004, ONGC along with SINOPEC negotiated a long-term deal with the National Iranian Oil Company for the development of Yadavaran, Iran's biggest onshore oil field. ONGC is likely to receive a 29% stake and SINOPEC a 51% stake. A related deal would allow ONGC to develop part of the South Pars natural gas field. If implemented in full the deals could be worth over $100 billion. The deal is still awaiting final approval (Congressional Research Service, October 2006 and International Oil Daily, February 5, 2007).

## Petronas (Malaysia)

- In September 1997, Petronas signed a $2 billion contract along with Gazprom and Total to develop phases 2 and 3 of the South Pars natural gas field. Petronas has since expanded its involvement to other portions of the South Pars fields (Congressional Research Service, August 2006).

### Petrobras (Brazil)

- In July 2004, Petrobras signed a $34 million deal to drill in the Iranian part of the Caspian Sea. In 2003, the National Iranian Oil Company granted the company a license to explore a 3,200-squaremile area of the Persian Gulf (Energy Information Agency, Department of Energy, August 2006).

### LG (South Korea)

- In September 2002, Iran signed a $1.6 billion development contract with South Korea's LG Construction to development phases 9 and 10 of the South Pars gas fields (Energy Information Agency, Department of Energy, August 2006).

### Norsk Hydro (Norway)

- In April 2000, Norsk Hydro signed an exploration service contract for Iran's Anaran block with the National Iranian Oil Company. In 2005, Hydro was announced as the winner of the tender for the Khorrama-bad exploration and development contract.
- In 2006, the $107 million contract was approved and signed with Hydro-Zagross, a subsidiary of Norway's Norsk Hydro ASA (NHY) (Congressional Research Service, August 2006).

### Statoil (Norway)

- In October 2002 Statoil signed an agreement with Iran to develop phases 6, 7, and 8 of South Pars gas field. The company reportedly plans to invest as much as $300 million in the $2.6 billion South Pars gas field (Energy Information Agency, Department of Energy, August 2006).
- Statoil is also working with the National Iranian Oil Company on improved oil recovery from 3 fields in Iran – Ahwaz, Marun and Bibi Hakimeh (Statoil 2003 Annual Report).
- In January 2007 China National Petroleum Corp (CNPC) began talks with Statoil to join a $3.6 billion project to develop the South Pars natural gas field (Dow Jones Newswires, January 12, 2007).

### China National Petroleum Corp (China) – Sheer Energy (Canada)

- In May 2002 Sheer Energy signed an $80 million to develop the Masjid-e-Soleyman (MIS)oil field. The China National Petroleum Corp (CNPC) then purchased the subsidiary of Sheer working on MIS. CNPC began work on the field in June 2005 (Energy Information Agency, Department of Energy, August 2006).
- In January 2007, the China National Petroleum Corp (CNPC), the coun-

try's biggest oil producer, signed a memorandum of understanding to invest $3.6 billion to develop a portion of the South Pars natural gas field. The MoU with Iran's oil ministry pledges CNPC to spend an estimated $1.8 billion on exploration and production in the SP14 gas block in the field and an additional $1.8 billion on building a liquefied natural gas plant. CNPC is in talks with Norway's Statoil ASA (STL.OS) about joining the SP14 project (Dow Jones Newswires, January 12, 2007).

### Bow Valley Iran Ltd. (Canada)
- In April 1999, Iran awarded Bow Valley a 15% stake to develop the offshore Balal field. Total and ENI are also invested in the field a reported total of $300 million (Congressional Research Service, August 2006).

### Gazprom (Russia)
- In September 1997, Gazprom signed a $2 billion contract along with Petronas and Total to develop phases 2 and 3 of the South Pars natural gas field (Congressional Research Service, August 2006).

### Lukoil (Russia)
- Lukoil and Norsk Hydro are involved in the exploration of the Anaran onshore project. Lukoil owns 25% of the geological exploration project (Hydro Press Release, September 29, 2003) .
- On February 18, 2006, Lukoil and the National Iranian Oil Company signed a contract for the joint geophysical and geological study of Moghan and Lali prospective blocks (Lukoil Press Release, January 18, 2007).

### GVA Consultants (Sweden)
- In March 2001, GVA Consultants, a Swedish company, signed a Caspian Sea transit contract worth an estimated $225 million. GVA was later acquired by Halliburton in November 2001. In March 2005, Halliburton said it would no longer take on new business in Iran (Congressional Research Service, August 2006).

### OMV (Austria)
- In October 2001, Repsol in conjunction with OMV, ENAP (through its subsidiary Sipetrol) signed an agreement to explore the Mehr oil block. In February 2007, the block was declared commercial with recoverable reserves of 150 million barrels (Platts Oilgram News, February 2, 2007).
- In June 2005 OMV reportedly signed a joint venture agreement for the planned 'Nabucco' pipeline project which would transport natural

gas from the Caspian Sea region to Middle – and West Europe. Other companies reportedly involved in the deal include Hungary's MOL, Romania's Transgaz, Turkey's Botas and Bulgaria's Bulgargaz. The construction cost of the pipeline is estimated at 4.6 billion euros (The Financial Times, June 27, 2006).

### ENAP (Chile)

- In October 2001, Repsol in conjunction with OMV, ENAP (through its subsidiary Sipetrol) signed an agreement to explore the Mehr oil block. In February 2007 the block was declared commercial with recoverable reserves of 150 million barrels.
- In May 2006, the state-owned oil company announced it would sell its 33% stake in the Mehr oil block due to the rising risk of doing business in Iran (Platts Oilgram News, February 2, 2007 and Global Insight, May 12, 2006).